A Retreat With Thomas Merton

Other titles in the
A Retreat With... *Series:*

A RETREAT WITH THOMAS MERTON

Becoming Who We Are

Dr. Anthony T. Padovano

St. Anthony Messenger Press

Cincinnati, Ohio

Cover illustration by Steve Erspamer, S.M.
Cover and book design by Mary Alfieri

ISBN 0-86716-229-5

Published by St. Anthony Messenger Press
Printed in the U.S.A.

Contents

Introducing A Retreat With...

Twenty years ago I made a weekend retreat at a Franciscan house on the coast of New Hampshire. The retreat director's opening talk was as lively as a long-range weather forecast. He told us how completely God loves each one of us—without benefit of lively anecdotes or fresh insights.

As the friar rambled on, my inner critic kept up a sotto voce commentary: "I've heard all this before." "Wish he'd say something new that I could chew on." "That poor man really doesn't have much to say." Ever hungry for manna yet untasted, I devalued any experience of hearing the same old thing.

After a good night's sleep, I awoke feeling as peaceful as a traveler who has at last arrived safely home. I walked across the room toward the closet. On the way I passed the sink with its small framed mirror on the wall above. Something caught my eye like an unexpected presence. I turned, saw the reflection in the mirror and said aloud, "No wonder he loves me!"

This involuntary affirmation stunned me. What or whom had I seen in the mirror? When I looked again, it was "just me," an ordinary person with a lower-than-average reservoir of self-esteem. But I knew that in the initial vision I had seen God-in-me breaking through like a sudden sunrise.

At that moment I knew what it meant to be made in the divine image. I understood right down to my size-eleven feet what it meant to be loved exactly as I was. Only later did I connect this revelation with one granted to the Trappist monk-writer Thomas Merton. As he reports in *Conjectures of a Guilty Bystander*, while standing all unsuspecting on a street corner one day, he was overwhelmed by the "joy of being...a member of a race in which God Himself became incarnate.... There is no way of telling people that they are all walking around shining like the sun."

As an absentminded homemaker may leave a wedding ring on the kitchen windowsill, so I have often mislaid this precious conviction. But I have never forgotten that particular retreat. It persuaded me that the Spirit rushes in where it will. Not even a boring director or a judgmental retreatant can withstand the "violent wind" that "fills the entire house" where we dwell in expectation (see Acts 2:2).

So why deny ourselves any opportunity to come aside awhile and rest on holy ground? Why not withdraw from the daily web that keeps us muddled and wound? Wordsworth's complaint is ours as well: "The world is too much with us." There is no flu shot to protect us from infection by the skepticism of the media, the greed of commerce, the alienating influence of technology. We need retreats as the deer needs the running stream.

An Invitation

This book and its companions in the *A Retreat With...* series from St. Anthony Messenger Press are designed to meet that need. They invite us to choose as director some of the most powerful, appealing and wise mentors our faith tradition has to offer.

Our directors come from many countries, historical

eras and schools of spirituality. At times they are teamed to sing in close harmony (for example, Francis de Sales, Jane de Chantal and Aelred of Rievaulx on spiritual friendship). Others are paired to kindle an illuminating fire from the friction of their differing views (such as Augustine of Hippo and Mary Magdalene on human sexuality). All have been chosen because, in their humanness and their holiness, they can help us grow in self-knowledge, discernment of God's will and maturity in the Spirit.

A Retreat With Thomas Merton: Becoming Who We Are holds a special place in our series. The author writes not as an unseen narrator but as a codirector of the retreat. Anthony Padovano's familiarity with Merton and his extensive experience in guiding Merton retreats enable him to speak of and for the Trappist monk in a singularly affective manner. For Padovano, "biography is spirituality." Thus, by sharing selected aspects of Merton's life story, the author invites us to get in touch with our own stories, our own spiritual journeys. He and Merton together are our companions on the seven-day journey that lies ahead.

Fittingly enough, as a motto for the authors of our series, we have borrowed the advice of Dom Frederick Dunne to the young Thomas Merton. Upon joining the Trappist monks, Merton wanted to sacrifice his writing activities lest they interfere with his contemplative vocation. Dom Frederick wisely advised the writer-monk, "Keep on writing books that make people love the spiritual life."

That is our motto. Our purpose is to foster (or strengthen) friendships between readers and retreat directors—friendships that feed the soul with wisdom, past and present. Like the scribe "trained for the kingdom of heaven," each author brings forth from his or her storeroom "what is new and what is old" (Matthew 13:52).

The Format

The pattern for each *A Retreat With...* remains the same; readers of one will be in familiar territory when they move on to the next. Each book is organized as a seven-session retreat that readers may adapt to their own schedules or to the needs of a group.

Day One begins with an anecdotal introduction called "Getting to Know Our Directors." Readers are given a telling glimpse of the guides with whom they will be sharing the retreat experience. A second section, "Placing Our Directors in Context," will enable retreatants to see the guides in their own historical, geographical, cultural and spiritual settings.

Having made the human link between seeker and guide, the authors go on to "Introducing Our Retreat Theme." This section clarifies how the guide(s) are especially suited to explore the theme and how the retreatant's spirituality can be nourished by it.

After an original "Opening Prayer" to breathe life into the day's reflection, the author, speaking with and through the mentor(s), will begin to spin out the theme. While focusing on the guide's own words and experience, the author may also draw on Scripture, tradition, literature, art, music, psychology or contemporary events to illuminate the path.

Each day's session is followed by reflection questions designed to challenge, affirm and guide the reader in integrating the theme into daily life. A "Closing Prayer" brings the session full circle and provides a spark of inspiration for the reader to harbor until the next session.

Days Two through Six begin with "Coming Together in the Spirit" and follow a format similar to Day One. Day Seven weaves the entire retreat together, encourages a continuation of the mentoring relationship and concludes with "Deepening Your Acquaintance," an envoi to live the theme by God's grace, the guidance of the director(s) and the retreatant's discernment. A closing section of Resources serves as a larder from which readers may draw enriching books, videos, cassettes and films.

We hope readers will experience at least one of those memorable "No wonder God loves me!" moments. And we hope that they will have "talked back" to the mentors, as good friends are wont to do.

A case in point: There was once a famous preacher who always drew a capacity crowd to the cathedral. Whenever he spoke, an eccentric old woman sat in the front pew directly beneath the pulpit. She took every opportunity to mumble complaints and contradictions— just loud enough for the preacher to catch the drift that he was not as wonderful as he was reputed to be. Others seated down front glowered at the woman and tried to shush her. But she went right on needling the preacher to her heart's content.

When the old woman died, the congregation was astounded at the depth and sincerity of the preacher's grief. Asked why he was so bereft, he responded, "Now who will help me to grow?"

All of our mentors in *A Retreat With...* are worthy guides. Yet none would seek retreatants who simply said, "Where you lead, I will follow. You're the expert." In truth, our directors provide only half the retreat's content. Readers themselves will generate the other half.

As general editor for this series, I pray that readers will, by their questions, comments, doubts and decision-making, fertilize the seeds our mentors have planted.

And may the Spirit of God rush in to give the growth.

Gloria Hutchinson
Series Editor
Conversion of Saint Paul, 1995

Getting to Know Our Director

Becoming companions on a journey is one of the most satisfying of human experiences. A journey makes us vulnerable, takes us from our more secure environments and commits us to the unknown. Perhaps this is why the journey has so often been our basic metaphor for life itself. Our life journey is a precarious pilgrimage, a passage through landscapes of promise and peril, a crossing from the darkness of the womb to the shadows of death. We travel in the hope that the light will not fail to guide us, that the star will not be lost, that homecoming will be granted and love not withheld.

To become companions on the journey of life or on the lesser excursions we make, it is imperative that we share with one another a word about ourselves. We do not wish to be led by strangers or by those who choose to be mute. Language is the bread of friendship, the communion of the heart, the wine which refreshes the spirit and brings us peace. When the word shared is gentle and loving, forgiving and healing, encouraging and honest, it begins a liturgy of life among those who share it. To receive such words is to receive God in syllables and silence.

And, so, you have every reason to ask who I am and I shall regard the question as an invitation and an obligation.

I am a Christian, always that, anointed in Baptism, Confirmation, ordination, all received as a commitment to Christ. These sacraments once given are irrevocable.

They are signs of an even deeper reality, discipleship with Christ.

I am a Catholic theologian, a writer of books, a maker of plays, a speaker around the world, a university professor in the United States.

I love people and I see God in human faces. My faith is rooted in the essential goodness of people, in their staggering capacity for love, in the gentleness of their dreams and the sturdiness of their hopes.

I have traveled the world, all the continents and most of the countries, and I have found God everywhere. I wrote my doctoral dissertation in theology on John Henry Newman and a doctoral dissertation in literature on Thomas Merton. Both men have been my life mentors. I have served in hospitals and parishes where one sees life journeys begin and end and I have learned from people about affection and pity, courage and endurance, and, yes, about the fragility and indestructibility of the human spirit.

I am no longer young, but I have not felt the aging, except, perhaps, in the tolerance I have learned and in my growing awareness that almost all human lives achieve their purpose and accomplish their destiny.

I believe that the losses in life serve a purpose and that people make few mistakes in their living. Most of what people see as a failure is little more than their inability to reach a goal that was often artificial and contrived. Many of our goals are forcibly imposed on our life by ourselves and others.

I am an optimist, convinced that there is far more good than evil in people and that the Church of Christ will never lose the gospel but will remain substantially true to it at the very core of its life.

DAY ONE
The Journey Begins

Introducing Our Retreat Theme

The theme of this retreat will be the spiritual journey of Thomas Merton and its relationship to our own era and our own lives. I shall trace the biography of Merton but deal with it in terms of the values and the vision it engendered. Merton's astonishing appeal to people derives from his ability to fuse his theology with his life and from his capacity to address the reader as though he were writing for no one else.

There are theologians whose biographies are incidental to interpreting their work. We do not need to know anything about Aquinas's life in order to appreciate his synthesis. The work of Merton, however, cannot be clear without some sense of his personal journey.

I have written extensively on Merton. Four particularly relevant publications of mine are the following: *The Human Journey: Thomas Merton, Symbol of a Century* (Doubleday, 1982); *Contemplation and Compassion* (Peter Pauper Press, 1984); *Winter Rain: A Play in Six Scenes* (Paulist Press Video, 1985); and *Conscience and Conflict* (Paulist Press, 1989).

I have taught courses on Merton at Fordham University and Notre Dame and given retreats around the country. I hope this personal introduction breaks the ice with those readers who do not already know me.

Opening Prayer

In his book *Thoughts in Solitude* Merton reveals that he is unsure about the journey, that he cannot see clearly ahead, that he does not know for certain where the journey will end or who he himself is.

When Merton wrote those words he had lived through seventeen years of monastic discipline and contemplative prayer as a Cistercian. It is helpful for us to reflect that if such a man could be confused or insecure, there is little reason to blame ourselves for our own perplexity.

Pause now and in silence consider these points:
1. To know the outcome of the journey is to trust God less.
2. If the Spirit leads us, the journey is not ours alone.
3. A journey of clarity and ease cannot reach a God of mystery and love.
4. The experience of uncertainty brings us closer to our companions on the journey.
5. No matter how unsettling the journey may be at times, God will not permit us to be lost.

Retreat Session One

A great war raged through Europe. It was said that this would be the last war in human history. The irony and the pity!

The horror of World War I reached surrealistic proportions in France, where once the Enlightenment promised everything and where cries of liberty, equality and solidarity had galvanized a continent and a century.

And now, the waste of it! France was crucified in barbed wire and trenches, lacerated and poisoned with gas and weapons. Humanity itself became a casualty and reason was mortally wounded.

It was in France, at just such a dark hour, that Thomas Merton was born on January 31, 1915, in Prades, in the shadow of the Pyrenees.

It was the war which compelled the impoverished Merton family to flee France. There may have been other causes. One cannot always discount Providence. Nor should we underestimate the iron will of the mother.

In any case, it was not an auspicious beginning.

Prades was not near the front, but the guns of August (1914) had made necessary a military hospital nearby. Soldiers passed in the streets on their way to death or slaughter.

Ruth Jenkins Merton saw to it that her husband, Owen, and her son Thomas would not be part of the carnage. They crossed the Atlantic and arrived in New York in August 1916, far from the guns of Europe.

Ruth Merton was an American, born in Ohio, the daughter of a publisher. She is described in the Bradford Academy yearbook as artistic and clever, a writer of poems and a dancer. Most of these talents will pass to her son. She loved France, its language, its art, its cuisine. Thomas will become fluent in French, a disciple of Jacques Maritain, one of France's more brilliant thinkers.

Ruth was a chronicler of life, a journal keeper. Her son is not yet two years old when she writes a record of his first months and of her sense of him. She notes his intense interest in words (later, he becomes a prolific writer). She speaks of his vivid dreams (he records his dreams regularly and carefully in his correspondence and journals). She observes that he is not patient and does not want to be held (Merton will lead a life of almost frenetic activity and, late in life, wonder why emotional bonding with women was so difficult for him).

One would speculate that mother and son were close. They seem similar in so many ways. She is a Quaker and abhors violence; he will be attracted to gentle people and peacemaking. Indeed, her husband, Owen, once wrote to a friend that his boy was like his wife in many ways.

Thomas remembers her differently. She is serious, anxious, impersonal, detached, demanding, cerebral, impatient, perfectionistic, critical of him.

People influence us in terms of the memory we have of them rather than in terms of who they were. Nonetheless, it is astonishing that the record of who she was seems so different from the son's memory of her. How can we explain this?

I believe it is due to two incidents, one of which Thomas knows, the second of which he suppresses.

The first deals with Ruth's dying and the way she parted from her son.

Ruth develops stomach cancer and dies in New York City when Thomas is six years of age. She was determined that he not see her weak, wasted, defeated. Her motives are not clear. Perhaps she was proud. Or perhaps it was a misguided act of love, a mother seeking to preserve her very young son from the trauma and the terror of the final stages. In any case, the departure permanently scars the son.

She refuses to let him see her. Instead she writes a letter when the end is imminent. Merton recalls the experience many years later, in his autobiography, with a vividness which astonishes the reader. It is clear that this occurrence never stopped occurring for him. Trauma is a wound which never heals.

Merton recalls that time in his life, a time of running in the woods with dogs, climbing trees, pestering chickens, watching his grandmother fire china in a kiln, convinced that none of this would end and that his mother would live forever. One day his father returns from the hospital and sadly gives his six-year-old a note. The first reaction is surprise, delight, pride that someone would write him and that he could receive a letter, like an adult.

But then he reads. His father leaves him alone. A mistake. Perhaps the father could not bear what was to follow. We cannot always manage what we know is necessary.

Thomas paints the scene. He is alone, in the backyard, under a maple tree, working over the letter, trying to decipher the words, unable to assimilate the meaning. He understands the sentences but tries to reject their import. His mother is near death. He will never see her again. This letter is their last communication. He must be good, remember what she taught him, do not miss her too much. She must say "good-bye." He must go on. She will not.

Merton describes his reactions: sadness, depression, no tears, and yet, grief as he had never known it.

Many years later, I interviewed James Fox, Merton's abbot for twenty of his twenty-seven years as a monk. He told me that Merton confided to him his sense of immense loss because his mother never allowed him to bid her farewell.

I believe that his harsh memory of his mother is refracted through this experience of parting and, perhaps, the toll the cancer had taken on her patience and emotions in the time before she was hospitalized.

There is another reason for the negative appraisal of his mother. It nothing to do with her. Merton, who writes so readily about his life, was never able to speak or write about this incident.

Not long after Ruth's death, Owen begins an affair with a famous novelist of the 1920's, a woman by the name of Evelyn Scott. They become lovers in the autumn of 1922, in Bermuda, while she continues to live in the same house with her husband, Cyril. This ménage-à-trois lasts for three years and fills the young Thomas with rage. We know this because Evelyn's son reveals it in his own autobiography and because Evelyn and Owen write about Thomas's strong dislike of his father's lover. Yet Merton never alludes to this. His sometimes shocking candor about himself will not permit openness in this instance.

Thomas is ten years old when the affair ends. It is possible that the negative response to his mother is due to some early memories of her, interpreted in their worst context by the letter she writes, and interlaced with painful recollections of the woman who took her place. It may not be logical for a young boy to make these connections, but he may have done it nonetheless.

We are devoting time to a careful review of Merton's life for the first three days of this retreat. We do so because biography is spirituality and because each life story has embedded in it a sacred history.

And what of Owen? Owen is Thomas's saint, his

guardian angel. The objective observer has other impressions, but they do not matter. The father is the son's memory of him.

Owen was born in New Zealand, studied in England and in France, and married Ruth (born the same year) in 1914 when each was twenty-seven years old. Owen dies of a brain tumor ten years after his wife's death. Ruth was thirty-four years old when she died; Owen dies in his forty-fourth year, when Thomas is sixteen.

Owen was absent a great deal during that decade. He followed the sun, painting bright pictures in Bermuda, northern Africa, southern Europe. And, of course, he was with Evelyn in a volatile and wounding relationship. There does not seem to have been much energy left for Thomas.

Nonetheless, when they are together something magical and mystical happens between them. The hunger of Thomas for a parent may have made more of those moments than might otherwise have happened.

Owen seems to have been a gentle man, loving poetry, music, painting and gardening. Thomas tells us he was more charitable than anyone else he had met.

Merton is devastated by his father's death. He recalls in later life the Byzantine Christ figures his father sketched as he lay dying. The sketches are startling because Owen favored landscapes in his painting and not portraits. These Christ figures, as we shall see, spark a major turning point in Thomas's life.

Thomas will combine the attributes of both parents, fuse the contradictions, live out the oppositions. He will absorb from his mother the pacifism and journal-writing, the love of language and the passion to chronicle life experiences. No matter that he was not kindly disposed to her. We are influenced not only by those to whom we are attracted but also by those from whom we distance ourselves. Owen Merton was an artist and sensitive to music, a restless traveler, someone who loved working with the earth, a free spirit. Thomas repeats these traits in his own life.

Two years after his father's death, Thomas travels to Rome. There he undergoes an experience which changes his life. It is not easy to understand exactly what happened. The result is clear but not the catalyst which brought it about.

Merton visits the churches of Rome and finds himself fascinated by Byzantine mosaics. One of those churches, Sts. Cosmas and Damian, is dominated by Christ in Judgment and the effect on Merton is electrifying. He feels the spiritual power that went into the making of those mosaics, senses the faith that inspired them, the dread, the sublimity, the anguish, the love. He begins to pray before the wisdom and the power of these figures. He reads the New Testament and shudders at the state of his soul. He is being led by a mysterious force, coaxed out of his self-indulgence, guided beyond the rebellious rage which seethes in him, a protest against the loss of parents and home.

The Byzantine sketches on his dying father's bed forged a link with the mosaics of Christ. He lights a candle for his father. He is acting in ways he cannot explain. He considers a candle for his mother but decides not. Even after her death, he is afraid of her. She could be so cutting, cold, harsh.

One night he returns to his hotel and turns on the lights. He is alone and he senses a presence. It is a flash, but he is overwhelmed. Something vivid, real, startling has happened, but he cannot discern what it is. He is filled with misery about the spiritual condition of his heart.

His father has been dead for two years, but he is

convinced that his father is in the room. He claims he is pierced by light, the language of mysticism. He is hungry for liberation. Urgency and anxiety shake him, though they have no clear object.

He prays as he has never prayed before, from the very roots of his being. It is a strong term, but it is his, the roots of his being.

He weeps intense tears. Through the blindness of his grief he realizes that his father is gone, but God is present. He prays from his flesh and bones.

When Merton writes his autobiography some fifteen years later, the experience is still sharp and vivid. He describes it with power and passion. His mind tries to dismiss the incident, but his emotions will not permit this. He is now a monk and has studied theology. The role he must play requires him to downplay the event. He wonders if he has made too much of that night. Perhaps his imagination was overwrought, his nerves were frayed. But this will not do. There was more to it than that.

He is certain of this much. He felt his father's presence, an interior light from God and grief about the condition of his soul.

This was the first of four ecstatic experiences Merton describes in his life journals. Each of them leads him to change direction dramatically. They come at critical moments and guide him correctly. This first experience is one of conversion to spiritual values. Eight years after this, he will enter the Abbey of Gethsemani.

There is one member of the family we have not mentioned. It is fitting to do so now.

John Paul was born in November 1918, almost four years after Thomas.

When Merton wrote *The Seven Storey Mountain*, John Paul had been dead some five years. He was killed in

World War II when he was twenty-four, in April 1943.
His plane developed icing and crashed into the English
Channel. He was picked up in a rubber dinghy, but his
back was broken. He survived a few hours, calling for
water, becoming delirious. He was dead long before the
rescuers came. His companions buried him at sea.

Merton's autobiography is filled with sadness and
guilt about John Paul. The hostility he felt for his brother
does not exceed normal sibling rivalry, but Thomas is
sensitive, the death is so early in their lives. The account
of their relationship is poignant, framed by two incidents.

In the first, Thomas is nine, John Paul five. His brother
seeks to come near a hut Thomas and his friends are
building. Thomas chases him with stones and John Paul
retreats, hurt, frightened, longing to be with his brother,
confused. The image lingers permanently in Merton's
mind.

The final incident occurs in July 1942. John Paul comes
to the abbey to visit Thomas. John Paul has decided to
become a Catholic. He still wants to be with Thomas, it
seems.

Merton describes seeing John Paul at a distance in the
abbey church where he could not reach him. John Paul
was in a high tribune. Merton signalled to his brother the
way around the building to a door which would admit
him. John Paul did not understand and had a look of
confusion which reminded Thomas of the time when they
were nine and five.

He sensed when they parted, they would never see
each other again. He was right.

The Thomas-John Paul relationship is important for
Merton.

The guilt Thomas felt for his younger brother
convinced him that he must become an advocate for all
those marginalized by people who have power. In his

poem, *Cables to the Ace*, he transfers the fall and original sin to the Cain-Abel story. Original sin, for Merton, is the refusal to care for the vulnerable. Merton becomes a prophet for social justice because he is determined not to be a guilty bystander, as the John Paul rejection is repeated with blacks and conscientious objectors, with the poor and innocent victims.

Merton writes one of his most touching poems to his dead brother and pledges to use his life to build a better world.

All our journeys begin as human journeys. It is only later that they become consciously spiritual. Our origins often hold the key to our future and form the core of our spirituality.

Merton once observed that he was in a state of ecstasy about the human race. It is an astonishing assertion for someone whose beginnings were painful. It is a central truth of Christianity that God became part of the human family. That is always where God is to be found.

For Reflection

- *Who was your mother? What was she like? How did she influence you? How do you differ from her? How are you similar?*

- *Who was your father? Do you wish he were different? What is your best memory of your father? Do you have memories less benign?*

- *What were your first images of God? If God became real for you when you were young, how did that happen?*

- *Who are your spiritual guides?*

- *Are you prepared to accept your life as sacred history?*

Closing Prayer

Reflect on the first steps in your life journey. We need to discover the grace, sometimes joyful, sometimes painful, in the concrete realities of our origins. It is time to be silent, to be grateful, to sense God's presence.

DAY TWO
The Valley of Despair

Coming Together in the Spirit

I remember him clearly. He was from Amsterdam, middle-aged, friendly, articulate. We met at a conference in Rome and had lunch together a few times. He was out of work, sponsored at this meeting by a group of friends who hoped the trip would give him some relief from the trauma of unemployment. Finding work proved difficult; he was not at an age when beginning again is easy or when employers find applicants attractive. It is a familiar story, too familiar.

"How do you spend your days?" I asked one day when the conversation had drifted into silence. "I look for work; I pray that I not lose hope; I walk an hour every day with my ten-year-old son." "It is not easy," I added. His reply has stayed with me through the years. "It is not easy, but I walk with my son. One day, when I am no longer here, my son will remember the walks we took and nothing else I have done for him will mean as much." We looked at each other and then quickly away, the way men do when emotions are intense.

In our losses, there is always grace. It is not a new or original idea. Sometimes we say it glibly. Stories remind us of how sturdy and valid a truth it is.

As we gather in the Spirit, we become ready to walk

with God and with one another. We find it hard to share time and presence when our lives are productive and successful. Such an irony!

Defining Our Thematic Context

We considered yesterday the beginnings of a young man's life, someone destined to become perhaps the century's most impressive spiritual guide. It was not an easy start. When the trauma was most intense, he felt the presence of God keenly for the first time and sensed his deceased father's nearness, the memory of the ten years they had together after the mother died.

Today we shall follow the young Merton into his valley of despair and we shall discover how he made his way through the shadows to find the light again.

Opening Prayer

In *Raids on the Unspeakable*, Merton reminds us that hope loses its innocence and its life when it rests on reason and calculation.

There is a tendency in modern life to equate hope with the measure of control we have over our lives. We believe God is with us when things go according to plan. Hope, however, requires a belief in possibilities which are not easily available or within reach. Hope remains even in the valley of darkness.

Be silent and reflect on the sources of our hope.

RETREAT SESSION TWO

Merton walked through a valley of despair and, at times, feared there was neither life nor light on the other side.

It was a time when all the world felt unsafe. Merton's life is punctuated with a bewildering succession of wars. In the 142 years from 1775 to 1917, America was involved in five wars (Revolutionary, 1812, Mexican, Civil, Spanish). In the 53 years of Merton's life, there were four wars (World War I, World War II, Korea, Vietnam).

Thomas was born six months after the guns of August (1914) began the worst conflict in human history to that time. His brother John Paul was born on November 2, 1918, nine days before the Armistice terminated the bloodshed.

Thomas entered the Abbey of Gethsemani on December 10, 1941, three days after the attack on Pearl Harbor.

The Seven Storey Mountain, which changed everything about Merton's life, was published in 1948. The Korean War began in 1950.

Merton died as the Vietnam conflict escalated. His body was shipped home with the remains of American soldiers killed in that engagement.

There is irony in the fact that a man identified with nonviolence, an apostle and prophet of pacifism should have had the parameters and, at times, the substance of his life defined by war.

And yet there may be a connection here. It may well have been the sense of irrational and inhumane loss, the massiveness and absurdity of the carnage that made nonviolence the only thinkable alternative.

In the fifty-three years of Merton's life, sixty-five million people were killed in war—more than a million, on average, for every year he lived. Among those losses was his brother, as we have seen. And, as we shall see, the woman and child he abandoned.

The human imagination collapses before the astronomical figure of sixty-five million deaths in some fifty years. The losses, however, are greater than this. One must calculate the toll on the surviving families and count the expenditure of human energy and planetary resources on weapons of destruction rather than on works of creativity and human improvement.

It was a time when all the major systems of the human community seemed to fail. The Depression marked the collapse of economic structures. Civilization itself seemed to lead nowhere except to the trenches of France and the bunkers of Berlin, to the Holocaust and Hiroshima, to Korea's Heartbreak Ridge and Vietnam's jungles.

If Merton came to doubt the capacity of technology to rescue us, he came by the doubt legitimately. Never before in all human history had efficiency and technology been harnessed on so massive a scale to destroy life and to corrupt its essential elements. In one war, poison gas made the very air we breathed lethal. In another, radioactivity contaminated the harvests of the earth.

Merton may have been primed for a negative reading of his era and his life by those tragedies in his immediate family which we reviewed in the previous session. Ruth Merton died when she was thirty-four and Thomas was six. Owen died when he was forty-four and Thomas was sixteen. John Paul was killed when he was twenty-four and Merton was twenty-seven. Thomas himself would die at the age of fifty-three, the longest-lived of his immediate family.

Ruth and Owen died of cancer of the stomach and the brain respectively. Merton worried most of his adult life about the onset of cancer. He was a candidate. There were no traces of it when he died at fifty-three, but had he lived longer, it may likely have developed. Merton could sometimes drift into hypochondria. A number of his illnesses were stress- and anxiety-related. It is easy to understand this tendency.

Two deaths are unnatural. John Paul is killed in a plane crash and Thomas dies of accidental electrocution.

It seems that death, on a global scale or in his family life, was a constant companion. It is not surprising, therefore, that his life inclines toward abusive behavior directed at himself and at others. He turns to alcohol and raucous protest, to promiscuity and defiance. He spends money compulsively and wanders relentlessly in a wild effort to find tranquility. There is no peace.

His behavior eventually takes a toll on other lives. A young woman companion becomes pregnant with his child and he abandons both of them. It is, perhaps, the single most destructive action of his life. He is filled with guilt, legitimately.

There are stories which rumor that the mother and child were killed in the bombing of England. They may be true, but the evidence is scarce. Even had they been killed, there could be no final relief for Thomas. He had to wonder through the years about the woman who bore his son and the son he never met. They surface obliquely in his final poem, the epic *Geography of Lograire*.

There were other problems. Thomas Bennett had been a friend of Owen Merton, and his physician. He was best man at the wedding of Ruth and Owen and, as far as we can tell, godfather at Thomas's baptism. Bennett is chosen by Owen to be Thomas's guardian when it becomes clear to him his own life is soon to end. Bennett, however, became more than legally responsible for Merton, at least in Thomas's mind. He was a surrogate father and Thomas transferred to him many of the hopes and some of the trust that had resided in his own father.

The behavior of Thomas causes Bennett escalating distress. He himself was a prestigious Harley Street, London, specialist, endowed with talent but short on patience. He was hardly the passive, quiet, accepting person Owen was. Thomas mistakenly assumed that one person would be just like the other, merely because they played similar roles.

As the relationship between the two deteriorates, Merton seems unaware of its gravity. Letters from Bennett become sharp and escalate in anger. Finally, there is a summons to come to London immediately. Thomas realizes that an impasse has been reached.

He is ushered into a waiting room when he arrives. He recalls the scene in *The Seven Storey Mountain* as an excruciatingly long period, and surmises that the duration is intended to punish him and break his spirit. The room is dismal, the atmosphere foggy, the magazines dreary, the time endless. In actual fact, he waits an hour and a half. In emotional time, it is much longer. He climbs, at last, a narrow stairway, feeling the confinement and sensing the impossibility of escape. The floor in Bennett's office is highly waxed and polished, adding to the precariousness of the situation. He almost falls as he makes his way to the distant desk. He is still a young man, not yet twenty, and he is thoroughly intimidated.

Bennett's attitude is lacerating. Merton describes his guardian as polished but cold, contemptuous, dismissive. The twenty-minute confrontation is one of the most painful experiences he has ever endured. In this demonstration of power, now he is the victim. Later, as he leaves the woman with whom he conceived a child, he will be the oppressor. Both experiences offer lessons that Merton absorbs.

He journeys from England to New York City. He writes a novel, *My Argument with the Gestapo*. It is smart, in the worst sense of that word: sour, negative, self-centered. He refuses to trust anyone anymore. Those on whom he depends abandon him, always abruptly, perhaps willingly, by death or design.

Merton began his novel as he heard of the bombing of London and other English cities. The novel is autobiographical. Twenty-seven years later, in the year he dies (1968), he refers to the novel as sardonic; he admits that Europe for him was falling apart and America was absurd, and that he had only contempt for both.

The novel is Merton's 1941 farewell to the world of illusion and hypocrisy. A problem lies in the fact that he sees no other kind of world. It is, therefore, a cynical book rather than an energizing one. Ten years after he wrote the novel, in 1951, he observes that he dismissed the world too summarily, ridiculing, cursing, rejecting. This, he adds, is no solution. He notes that denouncing the world is a way of making an exhibition of oneself and saying, in effect, that one is different and superior. In 1951, he is less smart, far wiser, more compassionate.

My Argument with the Gestapo is a strange book. Merton creates a fictional self, so close to the real Merton that he is named "Thomas Merton" and lives out experiences in England and France that are part of the real Merton's life. The book is a melange of dreams, imagined journeys, improbable conversations.

There are some powerful psychological mechanisms at work here. Merton is close to despair, not far, perhaps, from suicide. He tries to distance himself from his own life as he wanders confusedly through an urban and mental landscape of ruins and disaster. The main character of this novel is desperately lonely, disconnected, a victim of forces he can neither understand nor resist.

This is the only novel Merton did not destroy when he entered the Abbey of Gethsemani. He preserved it, I believe, because it said something about him not expressed anywhere else. It captures how near collapse he was and it gives us an insight into his conversion. The novel makes clear that at the deeper levels of his being his becoming a Catholic was neither tranquil nor optional. The alternative may well have been the end of his life. I shall suggest in a moment why Catholicism specifically was the choice he had to make. It is important, however, to add a word about this novel before we address that issue.

Merton describes himself as an exile and a stranger to every country in the world. He finds the world a prison and surmises that there is no purpose to his life. The only country to which he has a passport is "Casa." This allusion to home may well represent a veiled longing for the Abbey he will enter later that year.

Why then does Merton choose Catholicism in the turbulent, self-destructive experiences engulfing him? He chooses it, I believe, because of the optimism he finds in its tradition.

Protestant Christianity tends to be more pessimistic and more confrontative with the world. It is less tolerant and relaxed, more prophetic and accusatory, less humanistic and indulgent. Merton does not need this legitimate alternative at this point in his life. Orthodox Christianity is more remote and ethereal, more otherworldly and liturgical, less political and rational. He is not ready for this option now; that will come later. He turns to Catholicism because of its optimism and its humaneness, its literary and musical genius, its concrete and practical monastic traditions, its willingness to admit sin and not be discouraged. Its capacity to find the world a sacrament rather than an adversary is precisely what he needs. The sacramentality of the world does not mean that God is easily found in the world, but merely, as with all sacraments, that God is simply there. The sacramentality of the world requires that we not reject its materiality and limitations, but, as with all sacraments, that we transcend them. Transcending the world, however, in Catholic theology, means that we do not bypass it, a more likely Protestant inclination, but that we accept it and go through it. Protestant Christianity seeks an ideal Church; Catholicism is willing to live more easily with compromise.

Perhaps Catholicism gave Merton back his parents, first, by returning him to the love of letters which was important to his mother. This Church will be "Mother Church." Protestantism is less inclined to such a designation. In his final poem, *The Geography of Lograire*, Merton speaks of the Church as the woman who wants to nurture him.

Catholicism also allows Merton to value the painting and the music around which his father built his life. Catholicism permits him to believe in intermediaries and in the communion of saints, represented by his father's apparition; it offers mosaics and even Byzantine Christ figures; it revels in labor and the earth the way his father did. It is not surprising that the two religious communities Merton favored, the Franciscans and the Benedictine-Cistercians, had as their founding saints men who celebrated the earth in impassioned lyrics or in equating work with prayer. Catholicism convinced Merton that forgiveness, total forgiveness, is always within reach.

Merton turns to Dante at this period of his life, the Catholic poet who portrayed evil from the inside in the *Inferno* and yet wrote of Paradise in some of the most beautiful language ever written. It is no coincidence that Merton uses Dante's description of Purgatory as the title of his autobiography, *The Seven Storey Mountain*. Purgatory captures for Merton all the pain and evil of the world and yet allows hope. Dante tells us that only two differences divide Purgatory from the *Inferno*. The first of these is hope and the second is faith in paradise. Hope teaches that there is meaning in our losses. Paradise declares that life is more than the losses.

One day in the future, late in the journey, Merton will find Catholicism harsh, almost cruel, rigid and unyielding. But that is for another day, a later chapter in our book. For now, Catholicism is a beauty, ever ancient, ever new, which lights his path and saves his life. Catholicism gives him a concrete optimistic alternative, and it does this without endorsing Merton's sins and without allowing him to dwell on them.

It is never easy to calculate the losses of our lives. Sometimes the reverses are necessary to create opportunities for growth which could not happen without them. Indeed, the successes are not always advantages. Success is often an asset, but it has the capacity to define us and trap us. Success makes demands on us, creates expectations, imposes burdens on those we love and defeat on those we surpass. The elements which go into the equation of a human life and bring it happiness are not always balanced as we would have it. If the losses outnumber the successes, they may nonetheless prove more beneficial in the long run.

This we know: Merton suffered dreadful reverses. But this we also know: He became an unparalleled spiritual guide, a mystic, a writer of graceful prose and haunting poems, an inspiration to millions, a contemporary prophet who made nonviolence credible, conscientious objection possible, and social protest a spiritual path, even for contemplatives.

The valley of despair may have been necessary for all this to happen. Had there been only light, he might not have found the right road, or, having found it, might have wandered off it and treasured its direction less ardently.

We read in Merton's pain an insight into how we might judge our own. The Paschal Mystery may have been meant not only to assure us of life after death, but also, more concretely, to help us believe that happiness depends on losses more often than we realize, and survives those losses more convincingly than we suspect.

For Reflection

- *What have been the greatest losses of your life?*

- *Do you see possibilities in those defeats?*

- *Who and what rescued you when you were lost?*

- *What are your most ardent hopes?*

- *What makes you hopeful about them?*

Closing Prayer

Reflect on Gethsemane and the cross. Do not consider Easter, but view these events in their darkness and hopelessness. Had someone pointed to the dying Jesus and told us he would live again and that he would be remembered and loved through all human history, could we have believed it? His disciples did not. Should it not be easier for us to have hope in our own lives since our hopelessness is so much less than what Jesus encounters in his dying?

DAY THREE
A City Seated on a Hill

Coming Together in the Spirit

The flight from Seattle to New York was long and my
fellow passenger kept looking over to see what I was
reading. People are endlessly curious about the books
others take with them. The book in this case was a history
of Church and State in the Middle Ages. I assumed that
this person would see the title and studiously avoid
conversing with someone whose interests were exotic
and academic.

When lunch was served, he asked me if I were a
historian. I told him I was a theologian. He was in
international banking and was returning from Japan. I
tried to engage him in cultural comparisons and in the
adventure of travel and finance. He observed sadly that
he was unhappy with his life; he had always wanted to
become a history professor. His father would not pay for
his education unless he agreed to major in management
and business. His father controlled him and he allowed
the control.

Now he was wealthy, but the money had
overwhelmed his marriage. He had satisfied his father
but lost his dreams and the most vital relationships in his
life. One reaches a point, he noted, when the income
becomes addictive, the fear of starting over paralyzes,

and the alternatives seem impossible. There were long silences and halting words.

Because I was a theologian and a stranger, someone who might understand a passion for history, he revealed the pain he kept carefully hidden from others. The wounds inflicted by control and the loss of a dream were raw and sensitive.

He concluded, as we landed: "What bothers me is that travel is not exciting when it keeps you from your dream and never brings you home."

We parted. I had heard his story but could not heal him. People bear burdens with more bravery and courage than most realize. There is immense suffering in the world, anonymous, inarticulate. Jesus refers to the homeless and bereft in his description of judgment. Allowing people to find their way home is the heart and soul of Christianity.

Defining Our Thematic Context

We have followed Merton in his early journey, in his inability to find a home, even with his family. We then traced the sorrow which led him to grieve the loss and search for relief. At last, he finds the Abbey of Gethsemani and he experiences there the deepest peace he has known. He is twenty-six years old.

Today we shall survey the twenty-seven years he lived as a Cistercian monk. He is fifty-three when he dies. Slightly more than half those years form his monastic experience.

Opening Prayer

Home is first of all a state of mind and then it is a place. Home is the experience of authenticity and acceptance. We need to be who we are. Those who receive us become our community and our home.

Merton observes in *Seeds of Contemplation* that for him to be a saint, he must be himself. Nothing else is required.

The most fundamental of all our vocations is the calling God gives us to become ourselves. All else we do can be done as well or better by others, except this one and absolutely unique responsibility, to be who we must be.

To be oneself for a Christian involves connections with others, Church, Christ, God. These connections, however, must not make us false. Catholic teaching about the priority of conscience intends this: that one not be compelled to surrender one's integrity.

My fellow passenger on the plane felt homeless because his fundamental vocation to be himself, his very integrity and need for self-definition had been violated.

Merton is home when he arrives at the Abbey of Gethsemani because the illusions of false living were dispelled and he could be himself. He is able to be at home in Gethsemani because he is ready to accept it as home.

Sensing the presence of God, ask for enlightenment and pray for the grace to be committed to the vocation God has given you to be yourself. We need to reflect on how we might overcome our shortcomings, but first let us thank God for who we are.

It is time for silence.

Retreat Session Three

Merton was a monk of Gethsemani from 1941 to 1968. There is a natural progression in those years, I believe, from what I would call the monastic period (1941 to 1948), to the Church period (1948 to 1960), to the global period (1960 to 1968). The division is somewhat artificial, of course. All the years were monastic and they all related to the Church. Nonetheless, this arrangement has its advantages. The focus of Merton's attention is directed to diverse concerns as the years accumulate. A word about each of these periods may help us perceive the spiritual development they occasioned in Merton, the restlessness and creativity of his mind, the maturity of his self-understanding and of his calling.

Monastic Period (1941-1948)

Merton arrives at Gethsemani like a shipwrecked mariner reaching shore. He is twenty-six years of age, but he has lived through a fair amount of anguish, as we have seen. He has lost everyone, it seems, along the way. There will be further losses. But Gethsemani will anchor him, the way home and family do. When he rings the bell for admittance he realizes that he is coming home for the first time in his life and joining an intact family after so many years of rootlessness.

We are a bit ahead of our story and so we must consider the experiences and decisions which lead him to enter a Cistercian monastery. Granted the course of his life, this turn of events could not have been conjectured. How did it come to pass?

When Merton leaves Cambridge University and

England, he transfers to Columbia University in New York City. The University brings about a sea change. He encounters there his best friends and he keeps their friendship for life. There never was much doubt that Merton was talented and brilliant. He knew this. He did not, however, accept the fact that he was lovable and valuable in personal terms. For the next twenty-seven years of his life, friends will negotiate for him the terrain between his gifts and his worth.

Two professors foster his spiritual growth, one unintentionally, the other more directly. The Pulitzer Prize-winning poet Mark Van Doren becomes for Thomas a model of teaching excellence, literary eloquence and personal ethics. Van Doren becomes a surrogate father at a distance, a mentor and a guide, someone capable of receiving Merton's manuscripts, his honesty and his admiration.

The other professor is the philosopher Dan Walsh. Walsh is a brilliant teacher and a genuinely saintly man. Though idiosyncratic, he reads Merton rightly and introduces him to the Cistercians and Gethsemani. Walsh sees in Merton what everyone before him missed: Merton has a capacity for mystical and contemplative life.

There are other influences. He reads William Blake's poetry, writes his master's dissertation on it, and remembers how his father read Blake to him when he was a boy. He makes contact through Blake with a reality which transcends literature, time and the world as we know it.

Merton turns to unconventional reading: Huxley, Gilson, Augustine, Ignatius of Loyola. He is now a spiritual pilgrim. He finds hope in the possibility of his own purity of heart, believing in grace and magnanimity, in Christ and Catholicism, eventually in monasticism and priesthood.

He attends liturgies and finds a peace there he had never experienced. He reads the New Testament and resonates with its idealism and authenticity. Who could have believed he would accept such possibilities?

All is not smooth or easy. He still drinks too much. There is a swagger about him yet, masking insecurity and protecting him from vulnerability. He considers priesthood and dismisses it as impossible for him. Later, he will be refused by the Franciscans and others when he eventually does present himself as a candidate. His sexual history is checkered and the possibility of charges and legal suits from England is quite real. Merton endures one of the most lacerating rejections of his life. He is told bluntly that there is no place for someone like him in any of the Church's religious communities and certainly not in the priesthood. He wanders aimlessly after this, sobbing, choking. A goal once undesirable has become so important that its termination is unbearable.

On November 16, 1938, Thomas Merton was baptized a Catholic at Corpus Christi Church, near Columbia University. The Baptism was conditional since he had been baptized earlier. At this unecumenical time in Church history, baptisms done by other Christian communities were deemed doubtful at best. Merton's sponsor and godfather is Edward Rice. His witnesses are his other Columbia friends: Robert Lax, Robert Gerdy, Seymour Freedgood, all of them Jewish. He celebrates his Baptism in poetry and journals, and intuits, correctly, that the life of frenzied self-destructive behavior is behind him.

Merton travels to Cuba in 1940 and there undergoes his second ecstatic experience. He records it in *The Secular Journal*. It complements his 1933 vision of light with his father, the apparition that set him on his spiritual journey. In Cuba, priesthood and religious life become possibilities. His doubts about his worthiness are transformed into certitudes, ultimately unshakable, after this. Once again, this most intellectual of personalities settles his future on the level of emotional transcendence and mystical sensitivity.

Thomas describes the experience. He notes every detail. He participates in the liturgy in Havana, where a children's choir sings with clarity and feeling; a statue of Francis shows that saint offering himself to God; bells ring; there is silence; a young priest intones "*Credo*...I believe," and children's voices fill the church, loud, fervent, passionate.

Something goes off inside Merton like a thunderclap. It is his description. He sees with more than his eyes. He senses God, in power and glory, God, encircled by saints in song, God, with heaven itself surrounding Merton and the church building. Merton feels lifted from the earth, pierced with lightning, struck with thunder. There is no fear, only joy, beauty beyond all description, certitude with no hesitation.

A year later Merton journeys to Kentucky and asks the Cistercians to take him home. He delineates the scene in *The Seven Storey Mountain*.

He arrives in Louisville by train. He feels freedom in every fiber of his body. Distracted by joy, he wanders into a segregated waiting room filled with blacks. The atmosphere is tense, and Merton is apologetic. It is a telling coincidence. Later, Merton, from the stronghold of the abbey, will demand the end of this cruel and punishing system.

A stranger drives him to Gethsemani and then leaves him. The streets are empty and for a moment there is no one except himself, facing the abbey, summoning his courage. He rings the bell and hears it echo in the empty court beyond the gate. A brother eventually arrives and asks if he has come to stay. He answers, "Yes."

The monastic period is the time when Merton is involved with his interior life, when he is hidden in the monastery, anonymous. The vows of poverty, celibacy, obedience, the fasting and the silence, the prayer and the chant purify his heart. His poetry reflects the exuberance and the stillness.

This is a time of tranquility and joy, of lyrics and meditation. Without these years, these seeds of contemplation and creativity, the future would have been dissipated in motion without much substance.

These early years are the romance, engagement and honeymoon of religious life. The novitiate is a season of solace and celebration. It is an encounter with something safe, secure, apparently permanent. Merton feels the strength of the monastery and is ready to be lost in its larger reality.

He is known not as Thomas Merton, but as Brother (later, Father) Louis. There is rigor to his life that, at this point, suits him. There are intimations that his spirituality is self-punishing, harsh, almost savage. *Exile Ends in Glory*, his biography of a cloistered nun's life, was the sort of book—noncontroversial, pious—which Cistercian monks were expected to write, if they wrote at all. All this will change with *The Seven Storey Mountain* and Merton's writings on social justice. Merton endorses the inhuman asceticism of the cloistered nun and the arbitrary and cruel judgments of her superiors. The book is an insight into his life as well as into hers. He is not easy on himself. He must atone for years of drift and indulgence. He is seized by the zeal and extravagance of the convert. He is submissive and willing to let others define him. He is not unhappy, but he has banished for a time the nuance and ambiguity, the complexity and autonomy of maturity. These, too, lead to happiness, more comprehensively, but Merton does not yet see this.

He writes *Seeds of Contemplation*, a spiritual classic. The future germinates in him. The soil of his life is prepared for a harvest of creativity and glory.

The lyricism of these years is captured in his journal, *The Sign of Jonas*, especially its final pages, entitled "Fire Watch." The fire watch was taken in turn by the monks through the monastery late at night. The rounds were an effort to deal with any fires that might flare up while the monks were sleeping. Merton reflects on himself, his vocation, the meaning of life as he walks alone through the darkness of July 4, 1952.

The night is hot, almost beyond bearing. He catches the scent of bread in the deserted kitchen, the cotton of the tailor shop, the wet clothes in the laundry. He searches not just a group of buildings, but his own soul. He smells again the frozen straw of his first Christmas in the monastery. Only two weeks after his arrival, he celebrated the best Christmas of his life. He had nothing left in the world except God. He recalls his motives in coming to the monastery and weeps with shame. He looks at the church where his trembling voice uttered the vows that bound him to this community.

The night is filled with murmurs, the walls with traveling noises that rush and gibber in the distance. Finally, he achieves the door from the belfry to the roof. It swings open upon an endless sea of darkness. He wonders if death is like this. He stands higher than the treetops and walks in the shining blackness. He is cooled by the breeze of darkness, by the sight of distant stars. He prays with all his heart that he has not violated the silence by his books and letters, by the attention his work has brought the monastery, by the unworthiness of his presence.

It is a tender night that sheds light on the heart of a

mystic. He remembers that God hears our cries even before they are uttered and that God offers mercy and forgiveness before we have asked.

A dove begins a hushed flight from the stirring leaves. There is a faint light on the horizon. It is morning.

Church Period (1948-1960)

The Church period is inaugurated with a book which takes America by storm. It continues to reverberate throughout the world.

The Seven Storey Mountain is the narrative of a life and an era. It captured in 1948 the yearning for peace and the desire for faith occasioned by the ending of the most barbaric war in history. It portrayed a young man, in his early thirties, committed to something noble, permanent, stable. It was an anchor of strength in a world where certitudes and cities had been shattered.

For more than a decade after this, Merton wrote about spirituality and theology. He addressed an audience much wider than his fellow monks. He sought now to reach the whole Catholic world, especially the laity. In this last Catholic generation before Vatican II, in the quiet before the turbulence of reform and renewal, Merton composed books of piety which seem sentimental now, quaint, confined. One senses in them, however, beneath the surface, a tension ready to burst its limits.

The poetry of Merton takes on a different tone. It is conflicted, petulant at times. There is a trace of anger in it and, of course, ambiguity. The titles of his collections of poetry show this: *The Strange Islands*, *The Tears of the Blind Lions*, *Figures for an Apocalypse*.

Merton writes now for the whole Church, which has somehow become his monastery. He is a saint and a celebrity, both monk and mentor for millions of readers.

By the end of this period Merton is becoming Catholic by being catholic. He reaches out to Protestant Christians at a time when this reaching out was suspect. He finds boundaries, especially these, artificial. As a contemplative monk, he has less vested in the institutional structures of the official Church. He has grown considerably from his early books in theology (*The Ascent to Truth*) at the beginning of this period to books which strain the limits. He trusts, as mystics do, his intuitions and instincts. They tell him that Protestants are part of the Church, his brothers and sisters. They were once his parents.

The Catholic Church passes through a pivotal period as Merton ends this phase of his life. Pius XII's long papacy comes to an end in 1958 and a new Pope, John XXIII, brings a very different temper to the Church.

Merton is energized during these years by a sense of the Church he never had before the monastery. He had been a Catholic only three years when he entered Gethsemani. He knew a few Catholic priests and some of the social justice activists; he had read books, taught literature at St. Bonaventure University. The Abbey has given him a sense of the Church's long history, its traditions and theology. He becomes aware of the universality and longevity of Catholicism. He writes biographies of saints, chronicles of his own monastery, journals and poetry, prayers and meditations.

His autobiography brings a bewildering amount of correspondence into his life. This is a new experience. He becomes the recipient of the questions and hopes of tens of thousands of Catholics and other Christians. His consciousness is formed by the needs and stories of the laity and their relationship with the world.

It is the Church at large that prepares him for a global outreach and summons him to it. A pope in Rome speaks

of the signs of the times, of updating and *aggiornamento*,
of a Church that is more than medieval and Counter-
Reformation. Merton hears, and becomes simultaneously
a disciple and a leader. Until now he had seen the
universality of the Church and its unity in terms of
homogeneity and conformity: The world would be
served best if it were a Cistercian monastery or, at least, if
everyone were Catholic. Merton now discovers the
universality of the Church and its unity in diversity and
freedom. It is a new Pentecost for him.

Global Period (1960-1968)

These final years are breathtaking in their sweep.
Many of the themes we shall explore in the subsequent
days of this retreat come from this period.

We must discuss what seems a contradiction. This
new period is so different from what went before that
Merton becomes for the first time a controversial figure.
He will be censored by Church authorities, forbidden to
write on issues of peace and demilitarizing the world.
Until 1960, the idea of silencing a contemplative monk
would appear ludicrous—as foolish, perhaps, as a
Cistercian publishing works on the politics of social
justice and nuclear disarmament. More startling for many
was Merton's conviction that alternative world religions
and the passionate search for truth by sensitive
humanists could enlighten Catholics and bring them
spiritual wisdom. All this appeared to be a radical
departure, a betrayal perhaps, at the very least, a
misguided aberration.

On closer inspection, we can see that this period is
linked with what had happened before. Merton came to
the monastery after education in England, France,
Bermuda, America. He considered conscientious

objection as World War II approached, and worked in Harlem to alleviate the poverty and injustice of a system which degraded people. Some of his best friends were Jewish or nonbelievers; he had as mentors lay Catholics, often women like Catherine de Hueck and Dorothy Day, who functioned on the margins of institutional Catholicism, managing soup kitchens and criticizing all war as evil. He sought God in contemplation rather than in rote prayer, in the disadvantaged rather than in the privileged, in literature as well as in liturgy, in poetry and creative writing as well as in official doctrines and classic texts.

Merton is everywhere in these years. He writes of Hinduism and Zen, visits with Buddhists and rabbis, corresponds with atheists and revolutionaries. His books deal with war and technology, with racism and peace, with the immorality of the Vietnam conflict and the barbarism of nuclear weapons, with capitalism and Communism, literary criticism and calligraphy. He becomes a global figure, not as a well known Catholic monk, an ecclesiastical celebrity, but by defining himself as a companion on a journey which includes everyone.

The journey ends with his death in Thailand. It is a strange but instructive death in many ways, a witness and a symbol, an accident and yet fitting. There are so many anomalies.

The idea of a Cistercian monk on a pilgrimage through Asia, half a world away from his monastery, was not thinkable in 1941 when Thomas joined his community. That he should be there as an equal participant in an assembly of Buddhist and Catholic contemplatives could not be envisioned even at the end of his Church period in 1960. He dies there after giving a lecture on Marxism and monasticism, another improbability. He is accidentally electrocuted from faulty wiring that afternoon. The date is December 10, 1968, twenty-seven years to the day from his arrival at the Abbey as a young man of twenty-six. His life ends in Asia, where contemplation is often prized more than it is elsewhere in the world, in the east where the sun rises and endings are, therefore, easily symbolized as beginnings.

The spiritual journey of Merton from self and monastery to Church and Catholicism and then to the world and humanity is the pattern of the pilgrimage we all must take. It is imperative to pass through all the stages, to take all the steps so that the journey, when it ends, will have become inclusive and comprehensive.

To love God is to connect with everything. And so we must engage the self and the spiritual traditions of the local religious communities which attract us. We need to go into the catholic world of Christianity and find, in its expansiveness, a truth larger than our parochial and provincial insights. We are obliged eventually to embrace the whole world in its secularity and sacredness, to redeem it by loving it and to sanctify it by understanding it. In the final analysis, we come to know that God was incarnate in a heart that was human, so human that every person is able to feel the love and sense the acceptance.

For Reflection

- *What truths about yourself do you now affirm which you would not have accepted years ago?*

- *How has the experience of the Church expanded your horizons?*

- *Which values reach the whole human family and enable you to dialogue with everyone?*

- *Where do you feel most at home? With whom?*

- *How do you define yourself? What are your ultimate concerns? What lies at the core of your conscience?*

Closing Prayer

Remember the faces and names of those with whom you are at home. Recall the richness of Catholicism, its liturgy and sacraments, its heroic men and women, its better moments. There is glory, of course, not only in the Church, but also in the human community. We have been surrounded by people who have loved us and taught us, forgiven us and encouraged us. It is fitting to recall in silence the faces and names of those who have blessed us on our journey, those who still accompany us because of the memory we have of them and because of the influence they have had on us.

Day Four
The Desert of Solitude

Coming Together in the Spirit

The woman was dying. We both knew that. I was a young priest, on my first assignment, a chaplain at a hospital so large that pastoral relationships were difficult. A young priest is astonished at the confidence people have in him, a confidence not justified by competence or experience or wisdom, a confidence almost recklessly given. The confidence can help the priest measure up to it, compel him to become what people assume he is. The confidence is not in him but in what he represents; it is a trust not in one priest but in all those who preceded him.

"Is the baby dead?" she asked. I nodded and she turned wildly to the wall. Her young husband was a floor away. He did not know. I would have to tell him. Physicians worked feverishly to save her. I anointed her and she looked at me with sadness for all that might have been, with resignation at what could not be avoided and, astonishingly, with gratitude. She was grateful I was there, not, of course, because of who I was. She did not know my name. But because she was not alone and because I seemed to bring with me something more than myself.

We prayed until she lost consciousness. "God is my

Shepherd." So hard to accept now. She did. I wondered. "Though I walk through the darkest valley in the very shadows of death, I am not afraid." She became quiet. "You are always with me." In all this blood and agony? "And I will live in God's radiance forever." How much I want this to happen. She lost a baby, a marriage and her life. Only God is big enough to compensate for such losses.

Without the prayer, perhaps without me, she might have died in despair. The priesthood was worth everything it cost to prevent this young woman's dying in despair.

They tell me Jewish mothers, clutching their children in their arms, went into the gas chambers whispering: "God is my Shepherd. I have everything I need." I am prepared to believe it. Only death may rescue the words from mockery. The immense need and mystery of death make God believable. Not because we are desperate or terrified; surely we are. But because God requires vast neediness to be real. And the human heart obliges. A creator creates when the created has nothing to offer except the need to be.

I let go of her hand. It had no life in it. Life was elsewhere. I would have pulled her back had I the power and the means. But I was only a priest. All the poverty of the priesthood reached me then. I have never been so poor before or since. She had everything taken from her. And my caring could not salvage a single worthwhile keepsake from the shipwreck of her existence.

I went downstairs to meet her husband. I was no longer a young priest. I felt like a man whose life was over, tired, a survivor of all the lost battles people have waged since time began.

I broke his heart in a thousand pieces with the news. He wept in my arms. What did I know of loss? I would

never again believe that the priesthood required sacrifice.
How hollow the pretension! What did I know about
losing a child, a wife, a relationship, all in one moment,
all irretrievable, all announced by a stranger who knew
nothing of the love that had bound them together?

I shared with him the final words his deceased wife
heard, "God is my Shepherd...always with me...I am not
afraid." "How did she die?" "She believed the words and
died quietly."

Defining Our Thematic Context

We have followed Merton in his life journey. We have
tried to surface the themes and the accomplishments of a
significant life. As we noted in the beginning of this
retreat, the purpose we pursue is not biography but
spirituality.

It happens often that spirituality is judged to be
something at odds with one's life. For many, spirituality
is exotic, remote, contrived, artificial. Grace seems to be
granted by God only when we stop living the life we have
had. Merton apparently felt this way when he entered the
monastery. He burned his books, terminated his doctoral
study, intended never to write again, turned his back on
the world, and defined as reality only that part of the
planet occupied by Gethsemani, Kentucky.

He tells us that this monastery was the center of the
universe and that human meaning depends on what went
on there. It was a painfully narrow view of life. Those
who judge it harsh, unnecessary, unsuitable for
themselves or no more mature than some other ways of
living are not taken seriously by those who live it.

Later in his life Merton understood things differently.
He then judged *The Seven Storey Mountain* myopic and his

stance in it arrogant, bigoted. There are, we must admit, passages in the book which are painful to read; the dismissal of Protestants in general, the denigration of Anglicans, the discarding of Buddhism, the devaluation of the world community.

Of course, there is more than this.

However flawed *The Seven Storey Mountain* is in several of its parts, it is substantially on target in taking one's own life seriously and finding God in its development. Merton, through his journals and his autobiography, demonstrates that his life must not be taken lightly or for granted. It is, to this extent, a sacred history, worthy of reflection and able to astonish.

There was something Merton had yet to learn about the relationship between life and spirituality. Although he gravitated easily toward the idea that his life was significant, he still judged its significance by someone else's standard. It is true, of course, that other people may legitimately devise criteria by which we are measured, but these criteria monitor our behavior, not our self-definition. They may not take into account the growth that can follow the failures we make. We also grant that religious communities rightly reach into our inner selves and play a part in forming our belief, conscience and ethics.

Nonetheless, something else remains. It was this next stage which Merton took long to discover. He had to learn, as do we, that God is found in the core of our being; the substance of our life is, therefore, holy and sacred. The unfolding of our lives provides us with the revelation of God for us. The history of our existence is sacred and remains sacred even when we do not meet the criteria and even when our belief, conscience and ethics are defined differently by us from the definitions given by religious authorities. The fact that our existence is sacred, that its history is sacramental, does not guarantee that all we do is praiseworthy.

Karl Rahner, arguably the most profound Catholic theologian of this century, cautions us to love God and live life with the mind and heart we actually have, not with the mind and heart we are supposed to have.

In *Seeds of Contemplation*, Merton notes that we do not know how to pray if we never have distractions.

We often suppose that prayer is meant to be a perfect experience, that God expects us to be focused and unfailingly single-minded. This assumption is related to our attempt to live a perfect life. We have seen that our lives are sacred even if they are not flawless. A mother or a child may live a life which fills us with awe and reverence even if it is not without fault. A sunrise or a painting, a symphony or a dance need not be beyond all improvement; yet they may astonish us and bring us into the presence of the sacred, not far from absolute beauty.

Our lives are meant to be human lives. Our history, even when it is sacred, is intended to be a human history. And our prayer is best when it is a human prayer, a prayer from a heart that is not able to express itself without distraction or mixed motives.

John Henry Newman wrote about the demon of perfection. So much good is not done because people believe they must wait until they can do it perfectly. We demand, in turn, perfection from others, and are unwilling to accept as adequate or admirable, as sufficient or even extraordinary the efforts and achievements of those who might improve but who have already been significant.

These idealistic, utopian, even inhuman expectations may well defeat as much goodness as evil intentions do. It follows that we then want a perfect Church before we believe it and an inerrant Scripture before we accept it.

I have had no more unsettling experience in pastoral work than the confession by most people that they have lived inadequate lives, that they cannot believe that they are worthy and good, that God will not be easy with them because they have made so many mistakes. The dread of God which many experience, the vague guilt which accompanies their lives, the terror of being judged by God or others: All these derive from a diminished sense of our worth.

It is instructive to note that God, in Matthew's Gospel, judges the human family by surprising people with the revelation of how well they have lived their lives. Why do we extract from this account only the failure of those who have not met the standard for salvation? Should not the judgment of God be consoling? Why do we assume it will be harsh? Was not the message of Jesus good news?

Opening Prayer

Be silent. Consider, in prayer that is not perfect and in meditation that is not without unintentional distraction, the points developed here. Read through it again and lift your heart to God when you are moved to do so.

RETREAT SESSION FOUR

Prayer is a great mystery. It emerges from the secret depths of our hearts and convinces us that God is present, that we are able to reach God in the silence of our souls even without a word, that God receives the prayer and answers it.

Prayer comes spontaneously to the heart and lips when we are in crisis or when joy is more than we can contain or when tranquility brings us peace beyond all reason.

It is not easy to dismiss prayer as a fantasy. Jesus prayed. This we know. He prays in the mountains and fields, in great gladness when the disciples return after preaching, in frantic fear in Gethsemane. He prays on the Sea of Galilee, before the miracles, at the Last Supper when his words transform the meal, the bread, the wine, the sense of who we are and who he is. He prays people back to life, healing the desperate and desolate, bringing sight to a world without visions and hearing to communities without songs and speech, to people who do not know how to forgive. He prays and we walk again, no longer hobbled, on the path we thought we would never find. He prays and the darkness lifts, the nightmares end, the terrors cease.

He prays on the cross in agony so unbearable that death is an act of compassion. He prays at Emmaus as Easter bread is broken and on the shores of the lake when he prepares breakfast and the disciples rush to him in disbelief and faith.

It is not possible to be a disciple of Jesus and to fail to pray.

Francis of Assisi prays in the hills and in the sunlight, in the streets and villages, before the birds of the heavens and all the creatures God has made. Saints pray, as do the sinners. One cannot imagine an hour of human history when prayer was not formulated. Yet, we do not know how to explain it.

We have built temples so that people would have a place to pray and we have constructed simple shrines in the forests. People pray that they will find work, that the fields will yield a harvest, that a test will be passed and that a diagnosis will be favorable. Parents pray at the bedside of their children, when their sons are married and their daughters give birth, at the graveside of their grandchildren and in the final moments of their lives.

The world is encircled in prayer, every moment, and in all places. If we are blessed at times and do not know the source, if we feel sustained by a grace we cannot comprehend, it is with good reason. The planet has become a cathedral, a chorus of prayer, a sanctuary, a cloister where people retreat into silence and pray alone.

If somehow prayer were prohibited, if—worse—faith in its dominion vanished, if a time came when we relied on human resources and nothing else, the human family would feel the catastrophic loss and sense life draining from its limbs.

When I have told atheists I would pray for them, they were touched and grateful. When I read psalms for the dying, they were consoled even when they sensed that death could not be stopped. When I have promised believers in other faith traditions that I would remember them in the eucharistic liturgy, they saw me as their friend and brother. I cannot count the times when people said simply, "Pray for me," sometimes as an afterthought, often with emotions so strong they would look away or hold my hand or cry in my arms.

I, too, have requested prayers and felt blessed when others agreed. I have asked children just learning to speak to pray for me as well as the elderly who could no longer form words. I have asked rabbis and swamis, Buddhist monks and Muslim sufis to pray for me.

Prayer is a topic which has been handled glibly at times, disingenuously at others. It has been used to coax money from people and to control them. It sometimes is an exercise in superstition and an evasion of human responsibility. Prayer can be used to keep the oppressed in line and to justify the privileged and validate tyrants and inquisitors. But this is not prayer, only the mask exploiters wear when their intentions cannot bear the light of day.

Merton prayed a great deal. He sought to understand prayer, but he was not much better at fully explaining it than anyone else has been. Nonetheless, he offered some insights and shared arresting thoughts.

Six particularly clarifying principles Merton espoused have helped me see prayer in a new light.

Prayer happens in accord with the beliefs or assumptions we make about life. Some of Merton's principles were an effort to verbalize his own suppositions.

The first principle is this: Sanctity is nothing more than becoming ourselves. This is a liberating idea.

People who have no faith in their own life, who secretly hate who they are and what they have accomplished, are the first to reject Merton's call to become ourselves. They feel that attempting to become ourselves guarantees narcissism. My experience has been that the most self-preoccupied people I have known are those who despair of their lives.

In any case, Merton reduces spirituality to a simple formula: Become who you are, who you are meant to be. We explored this theme in our last session. We see it now as a prelude to prayer and we use it to connect Merton's life story with his theology and spiritual doctrine.

The second principle is akin to the first. Merton observes that effort and difficulty are adversaries of spiritual development.

Artificial prayer, contrived spiritual systems, are like forced conversation. They are all burden and no communication. They are self-conscious in the worst sense. Conversation works best when we are not self-aware, but are lost in the joy of communicating. Conversation and conversion are practically the same word. One of Merton's best journals is entitled *A Vow of Conversation*. These few words express his whole spiritual life.

Denial, discipline, sacrifice should be natural, spontaneous. They are the companions of a responsible life, the inevitable consequences of commitment, the unavoidable concomitants of dedication. Freely chosen asceticism is, for Merton, often theatrical, artificial, a stratagem to call attention to the self. Strenuous, self-inflicted effort easily becomes a search for our own devotion in place of God, a gaudy manifestation of our own goodness rather than a quiet acceptance of our worth. Our harsh punishments do not lead us to behold the face of God but the mirror image of ourselves.

The third principle is the acceptance of vulnerability. Love is made strong when it is unafraid of its own need, not scandalized by its insufficiency, neither terrified by how much it is dependent on others, nor eager to preserve the dependency. Vulnerability is another word for incarnation, an essential component of our humanness. To deny our vulnerability or to mask it is to camouflage our humanity. Vulnerability does not mean self-pity or histrionic woundedness. It is merely the allowance of pain in our lives when the task at hand or the self-definition permit no alternatives. Vulnerability is the human cost of our existence.

A fourth principle is acceptance of where we are in life. Again, these principles can be misunderstood. Properly perceived they are liberating; misapplied they are destructive. Merton does not intend that we become fixated, paralyzed in the situation in which we find ourselves. Even the change we are obliged to make is an acceptance of where we are.

As a monk in the Benedictine tradition, Merton knew about stability and valued it; as an American, he was aware of excessive mobility, restlessness as an illusion, change as a mirage, novelty as an evasion. Too much work and too much diversity, too many successes and an endless pursuit of one achievement after the other: All this is an attempt to justify a life in which we no longer believe. We create a false self and invite people to consider our record rather than our heart, our résumé in place of our presence.

Merton insists that we can grow where we are, that the next stage is often equally disadvantageous or worse. At some point, we must cease and recognize that our humanity is limited. It is destructive to live in the illusion that all things are possible and no losses need be admitted. The power of positive thinking does not work if it is not, after all, thinking.

A fifth principle is premised on the capacity of the human emotions to aid our spiritual life. Violence is a human emotion, but it is an expression of our emotional immaturity. We sometimes use violence to repress our own emotions or those of others. Unworthy emotions, however, are resisted by expanding our human horizons. Perhaps it will help to make this less abstract.

Merton believes that sexual temptation or envy or anger can often be brought into line, not by attacking them violently and seeking to repress them, but by making our life emotionally richer. An opera or a museum exhibit, a walk in the woods or a symphony may lift us out of self-destructive tendencies and unethical behavior more readily than harsh asceticism, frenzied prayer, self-punishment. Merton believes that sinful temptations are the result of a diminished view of life. He prefers emotional enrichment to self-punishment. A need to punish the self passes quickly into a need to punish others.

The sixth principle invites us to reject the tendency to organize our life rigidly. People involved in religious and spiritual searches are often so inclined. Rigidity is not a sign of life. Merton observes that when a shoe fits, the foot is forgotten. When the shoe is rigid, tight, the foot is an object of preoccupation.

The spiritual life is an experience of letting go, an act of trust in the rhythm of the universe, a cosmic dance, a divine comedy in which grace increases the more it is refused. The spiritual life is music and melody, an achievement which makes us one with ourselves and with all others. It is as natural as a song which enchants, as life-giving and effortless as the beating of our hearts.

These six principles are Merton's effort to make the spiritual life and prayer simple and available to all. A hallmark of truth is its simplicity; a characteristic of artificiality is its complexity. For many, the notion of prayer and the spiritual life is convoluted, contrived, inaccessible. Merton's mission was to bring contemplation to the average person, to reveal the mystical potential in our own hearts.

Jesus did not strain to be who he was. He does not teach in a tangled, cryptic manner, but by means of stories and parables open to everyone. Jesus does not intend a spiritual life for the elite, one managed by a religious system which forever makes people dependent on it.

The strategy Merton adopts to accomplish his task is the development of principles such as those we have explored. For the person attracted to the spiritual life but intimidated by its requirements, Merton is enormously helpful. Merton noted that the contemplative monk justifies his position by bringing to people insights they are not likely to realize on their own. Merton feared that if the monk does not do this he will live a life of monastic self-indulgence, exotic, privileged, secure, idiosyncratic.

Merton showed how fitting it was to have a spiritual life and that this did not necessitate neglecting the commitments and responsibilities of everyday life. His message was compellingly simple and wise: Be yourself; let asceticism emerge from the way you live; do not seek or avoid vulnerability; become peaceful wherever you are; develop your emotional horizons; do not organize and program life rigidly.

From these principles, a number of practical consequences for prayer followed.

We have seen already that Merton did not consider distraction disruptive of our prayer life. Indeed, he suggested that prayer without distractions was not only unnatural but undesirable. When the human mind is limited to one thought or the human spirit is driven by one preoccupation, life is not simplified but brutalized.

Prayer is supported by some structure or system, some regularity, just as life needs some degree of order. But prayer must always remain personal. The structure and the frequency, the duration and the form one utilizes should be dictated by one's personality and life-style. Lay people should not follow monastic conventions in prayer.

In any case, prayer is a means to an end. Christians are not expected to take prayer seriously but to take God seriously. If one loves God, one learns how to pray. Jesus took God seriously in his preaching, but spent little time teaching people to pray. If we get a relationship right, we usually know what to say in it. And we say what needs to be said in our own manner. There are, granted, things to learn about communicating, even with those we love. But technique in communicating will not assure a good relationship.

It was in the fifteenth and sixteenth centuries, Merton

maintains, that we began to formalize prayer and suggest uniform approaches to it. Theologians and spiritual writers were influenced by the scientific method and laboratory experiments. They, too, searched for laws that were general and universally applicable in the same way to all. Some forms of prayer were approved as true, alternatives were discouraged as less effective.

Prayer is not science, Merton argues, but poetry. Poetry does not value the general law (all nightingales, for example) but the specific instance (*this* nightingale). Prayer is closer to the child's fascination with the particular, individualized manifestation of reality than with the adult's effort to create a general context. We need both perceptions in order to get on in life, but as far as prayer is concerned, the poet and the child in us may be more useful.

Prayer flourishes when we appreciate our senses and emotions. Like all relationship, prayer is not as much a cognitive endeavor as an intuitive experience. It is more akin to lyric than logic. It emerges from our subconscious.

In the first of the principles Merton gave us, he insisted on the correlation of sanctity with becoming ourselves. We can see now the application to prayer. If we expend our spiritual energy in trying to become something we are not, we shall find prayer tedious and exhausting. The empirical or inauthentic self prays in a manner which is neither genuine nor personal.

Merton tells us in other principles that a narrow focus makes us violent with ourselves; a rigid organization of our existence destroys the spontaneity and the joy. All this affects our prayer. Hemmed in, we become punishing with ourselves as well as with others. We might pray a great deal, so to speak, but, since it is not truly prayer, we seem bitter, angry, judgmental, cruel. We have all met people like this. Some suppose they are saintly, but those who know them think otherwise.

Prayer should not be used, Merton writes, to dominate others and control them. It is difficult to understand how we could have prayed for the success of the Crusades or prayed during the Inquisition even as we tortured and burned the heretics.

Prayer, however, is a joyful experience when we enter into its essence. It enables us to preserve a childlike vision in our maturity, a poet's youthfulness in our aging. Prayer prevents our life from being dissipated in frenzy and illusion, in pettiness and rage, in deceptiveness and vengeance.

It is impossible for a believer not to pray. As the Quaker hymn asks: "How can I keep from singing?" Properly understood, prayer is the song of life.

For Reflection

- *How were you taught to pray?*

- *When and how have you prayed best?*

- *Did these successful moments in prayer follow the traditional approach to prayer you were taught?*

- *How is it best to teach children about prayer?*

- *Do you need some structure in your prayer life and what might that be?*

- *Where are you most vulnerable in life and how might this vulnerability help your prayer?*

- *Do you assume that your life would have more meaning if it were better organized?*

- *Do you tend to take prayer more seriously than God?*

Closing Prayer

This is a time to apply some of our insights on prayer.

Begin by reflecting on who God is for you. Be gentle with yourself and honest. Suppose that there were no longer a Church. We would be left on our own to define who God is and how we might relate to God.

Suppose further that there is no longer a circle of friends, family and responsibilities. We are asked to define who we are and what we would like to become in our lives.

What is God like, what are we like, when other people's definitions of God and ourselves do not intrude?

You will discover in your meditation that when we have reached some insight and resolution on who God is and who we are, we shall seek the Church and our circle of companions. We come now, however, with more to offer.

Let us pray:

Gracious God, give us the grace to pray, not so that we may pray better but so that we may love more. Enable our prayer to set us free so that we may find you in passion and peace, embracing others in joy and generosity. You are the God who taught us to speak, who gave us your Word, who heard our silence. Teach us to pray now so that our speech will be honest, and our silence a melody of love.

Day Five
New-found Land

Coming Together in the Spirit

If I mention his name you might know him.

The story he has to tell us does not require his identity. Like all good stories, it is ours as well as his once we hear it and accept its truth.

Even though our storyteller has no name, it might be useful to share some details about his life. The details may help, partly because the story is true in a factual as well as a mythic way, and partly because the details provide a context and a measure of explanation.

His career led him to Washington, D.C. It was a successful career. I met him when it was over. It is important to know why the career ended.

If I tell you three items of information you will know how prominent and promising he once was. He worked for the State Department as an adviser to Henry Kissinger. I ask you not to let your value judgments or politically partisan preferences get in the way of seeing these components as elements in a successful career. On a résumé, they would get attention. We know this.

At some point in his ascent, doubts emerged. They were not doubts about his ability to function in the rarefied atmosphere, nor hesitations about his capacity to climb higher. Who could say where this would end? Nor did he experience a failure in desire or ambition. His competitive spirit was strong and his talent to sustain it seemingly inexhaustible.

Why, then, did he have doubts?

His doubts clustered around questions concerning the worthiness of the effort and the ethical character of the climb.

We must not become accusatory or judgmental about the city, the Department, the Secretary of State. This is a story, not an indictment. Since it is also our story, it must raise for us questions about the worthiness of our goals and the ethical compromises we may have made along the way. Honest men and women are not intimidated by the questions or where they may lead.

In any case, heroism was required from a man who knew he was talented in many ways, but not certain that ethical heroism was one of those ways.

Grace is given, we believe, to those who do not expect it and have not even asked for it.

He resigned his position. It is easy for those who have not achieved such heights to make less of his descent than they should. Every climber knows that the most wrenching of disappointments is turning away from the summit, especially when one knows it was possible, in sight, and that one has the ability to continue. When circumstances, not incapacity, make the descent imperative, the loss of the summit is especially bitter.

In any case, the glitter and the glory were gone. The ordinariness of life after the decline was not an easy adjustment. But it was finished. And my friend needed to accept that fully.

There was one particularly painful experience in his departure. The leavetaking was acrimonious. There were charges of betrayal. When explanations were demanded, they came across as indictments, even though this was not the speaker's intention.

You have many of the details now. They are important, as we shall see.

Not long after his resignation my friend was summoned by the Internal Revenue Service for an exhaustive tax audit. It may have been a coincidence. One wonders.

The auditor, a woman, seemed to conduct the audit with a prearranged agenda. It was not easy.

The tax laws are so complex that IRS auditors, called by telephone in a random sample, often give different and contradictory answers to the same question. If an auditor is intent enough on finding fault, many taxpayers will falter.

My friend was an honest man, intelligent and articulate. He was talented, as we have said, in many ways. Finances and accounting, tax returns and recordkeeping were not among his gifts.

And so he lost in this revenue end-game. He was not a wealthy man. The loss was nerve-wracking not only because of the financial dimensions but because he suspected it was unjust, discriminatory, capricious, punishing. He was not a citizen under review but a victim who had been carefully targeted.

The audit left him financially distressed. As he departed the tax offices, he was angry, astonished at the violence of the language surging through him. Had he learned the woman in question had suffered a calamity he would feel no pity; indeed, his reaction might be one of satisfaction.

As my friend reached the street, the fresh air cleared his head. He knew that what he felt was poisonous, but he seemed unable to stem the rush of malice.

Abraham Lincoln spoke of the better angels in our nature. Others might speak of prior conditioning or of grace, of Providence or of reason. No matter the source, something wholly unexpected turned him around. He felt revulsion about what was happening to him, the ugliness of it, the demonic frenzy, the irresistible force which shook out of him the last vestiges of his humanity. He spoke to himself, an interior dialogue with his lesser nature and his greater self. How could he, a proponent of nonviolence, so recently a witness against the unethical decisions of his colleagues and supervisors, how could he, in a few hours, be transformed from compassion to fury?

He noticed that the force of the debate with himself had stopped his walking. He had been standing still for a period of time he could not measure. He looked around and wondered whether he had become an object of attention. He noticed he had been standing in front of a florist.

Now, the thought broke into his consciousness, like a flash of lightning across the horizon. He entered the shop and spent a not inconsiderable sum of money on an arrangement which was as beautiful as any he had ever seen or purchased.

He retraced his steps and entered the IRS offices. The woman auditor was, fortunately, between clients. She had not seen him enter. He crossed to her desk.

"I brought some flowers for you."

"I don't understand. Why are you doing this?"

"I need to do something generous now. It is part of my religious sense of things."

"Is this a bribe to have me reopen your audit?"

"No, I accept the audit; I do not want it revisited; I cannot handle any more stress in that regard."

"Are these flowers your attempt to meet me outside this office?"

"I am a married man, happily married. I shall explain

the flowers to my wife. Most likely we shall not see each other again."

The flowers, the unusual behavior of a client returning, the conversation attracted attention.

The auditor continued as her supervisor approached.

"Why, then, are you doing this?"

"I know it must be difficult to have an adversarial relationship with people on a daily basis. I sometimes had to work that way at the State Department. You and I had a long, hostile interview. I need to do this for me as well as for you. Please accept the flowers."

The woman turned to her supervisor.

"Do you see a problem here?"

"Only if he wants his audit reconsidered."

Turning to my friend, the supervisor asked if that was his intention.

"No, I accept the audit."

"Tell me why you are doing this."

"I recently resigned my job. I was troubled by the way people deal with each other. I felt very angry as I left this office. I did not want to let that anger consume me. It is not easy to explain. This is something I must do. Would you allow this woman to accept these flowers? I will, most likely, never see her or you again."

There was a moment of silence. The supervisor agreed, the auditor took the flowers, my friend left.

He told me that the money he spent was a wise investment in his own life. In an instant he freed himself from weeks of rage and recrimination. The animosity would have gained him nothing. The audit would not be altered.

There is a possibility that the woman auditor was changed by this act of generosity from an unexpected source in some substantial way. My friend allowed the supervisor and the office staff to see human behavior at its best. Such a witness bears its own fruit.

Nonviolence is dismissed by some as unworkable. There are those who will read this account and say they are not capable of kindness under attack. It is not easy to think of a better way to have handled this situation. Everyone gained, not only those who were participants in this drama but those countless others who read or hear the story and those with whom they share it. It is seldom that a relatively small sum of money—a considerable sum at the moment but inconsequential in the long run—is spent so well.

Defining Our Thematic Context

We are about to follow Thomas Merton into what we have called a new-found land. It is the land of pacifism, peacemaking, nonviolence, conflict resolutions.

We have followed Merton on his life journey. Our first three sessions surveyed the chronology and highlighted the values and the lessons. We were his companions as the journey began and the first steps taken. We walked by his side in the valley of despair, at a stage in the passage when promise turned to ashes and death emerged on every side. When all might have failed, even life itself, a city on a hill offered hope. The city is a metaphor for the Abbey of Gethsemani. Merton found a home and was nurtured back to life. He was given sanctuary when the burden of the journey was more than he could bear and when all the world seemed a wasteland.

The life of Merton is a parable. Like all parables, there is a spiritual lesson in it. Like all parables, it is someone else's story and our story at one and the same time.

In our fourth session we turned to other matters. We began our development of themes in Merton's writings.

We began with prayer, since this is often where the spiritual dimension of our life journey is set. We take up in this session the vision of creating a world in which violence has no place. Less grand than the whole world but no less urgent is the possibility of living at least our life without assaulting others, the environment, ourselves.

It is important to note that the nonviolence of Merton is part and parcel of the entire journey. It is also inseparable from prayer. We cannot become nonviolent without reflecting on our own life. Nonviolence, Merton maintains, is not a strategy, a technique, even a specific choice. Nonviolence is an entire life. It is the self transposed into another key. Nonviolence is supported powerfully by prayer and the conviction it brings that justice is assured in the long run. Prayer helps one realize that there is a law of compensation in the spiritual order of things, that the losses are restored and the truth secured.

We saw in our last session that the value we attach to prayer has something to do with the vision of life which guides us. This is also valid with nonviolence. Martin Luther King once suggested that unless people were convinced history was on the side of justice they ought to leave the civil rights movement. For, he maintained, their pessimism will bring violence with it.

I believe nonviolence is the hallmark of contemporary spirituality, the touchstone and measure of its authenticity and depth. It is, therefore, urgent to consider Merton's views on this theme and our own choices in this regard.

Opening Prayer

The essence of the world's major religions rests in compassion for the earth and for others. No religion makes a virtue of enmity or rejects reconciliation. A world of peace is the energizing vision for religion. It is the great mythic dream for the human family. Most parents want their children to grow up in a world with no more violence.

Meditate about why we ardently want such a world. Does it not have something to do with our seeing violence as ugly?

How did you respond as I related the story at the beginning of this session? If you were moved and inspired, might it not have been because we know in our heart of hearts that human beings behave this way when they are at their best?

Had Jesus died doing violence, would we still remember him? If Francis of Assisi sought revenge on those who injured him, would he inspire the world as he does? If Teresa of Avila or Thérèse of Lisieux had been women of violence, could they reach our hearts as deeply as they do? When we admire our parents, do we tell others stories of when they were violent or of when they were kind?

Let us pray.

Gentle God, you are defined as love itself. The Scriptures proclaim the love with which you created the universe and the love you affirmed on the cross. Bless us so that we may become disciples of your love and bring love into those places in the world where love is denied. Amen.

RETREAT SESSION FIVE

We suggested earlier that Merton's nonviolence may have had its beginnings in his mother's convictions and his father's approach to life. He gravitated in this direction easily, writing about Gandhi while in secondary school in England, analyzing the poetry and mysticism of Blake while in graduate school. He found conscientious objection convincing in the time before World War II when it had little social support. He was drawn to pursue a life with the Franciscans and to become a monk of the Abbey of Gethsemani. Nonviolence was always there, it seemed, on the life agenda of Merton's concerns.

Merton wrote about nonviolence regularly, seeking to explain its import to himself and others. He encountered resistance as he criticized war and weaponry. His intent was not political, but brought inevitable consequences.

Pacifism was the natural fruit of Merton's contemplation and his study of the Church's history. He took exception to Augustine's just-war theory. Augustine argued that it was possible to kill others morally, if one intended objectives other than the killing, and if war were the last resort.

Augustine's position made sense, Merton maintained, in the rational order, but was untenable in the real or existential order. The sharp divorce between intention and behavior creates a moral schizophrenia in which one's motives are separated from one's actions, in this case, killing a human being. Augustine's thinking permitted the Crusades and the Inquisition.

Merton had learned from Gandhi the spiritual discipline of genuine pacifism. The disciple of nonviolence must be as concerned about the adversary as about the self. Nonviolence seeks to liberate the adversary from the mentality which makes violence and oppression appealing. It seeks to renew and reform a situation radically, not by having oppressor and oppressed merely change places, but by eliminating oppression altogether. In its finest expression, nonviolence allows all to win.

Merton felt that the gospel and early Church Tradition imposed on Christians the imperative of nonviolence. Clement of Alexandria observed that a disciple of Christ is a soldier of peace in an army that sheds no blood. Justin concluded that a Christian does not take another's life but dies for Christ. Tertullian, with his striking way of writing, insisted that Jesus disarmed every Christian soldier when he told Peter to put away his sword.

Nonviolence imposes the need to root out our fascination for total solutions to problems and totalitarian approaches to life. We become violent because we believe we alone have the answers and the truth. We conclude that alternatives to our position must make matters worse and be false. There is arrogance in this.

Truth is not an abstraction. It abides in people and in communities. To destroy people for the sake of an objective truth is to make the truth an idol rather than a means to love.

Christians become belligerent, Merton affirmed, because they see the truth as smaller than they are, as something less significant than the Church. No, Merton thundered. The truth is larger than we are. It endures even when we do not defend it. We are not the possessors of truth but its servants. The truth is more than we are, more than the Church is. The Church is a minister to the truth, a witness to it, not its master.

If we believe that the truth is invincible, then we do

not attack others to preserve it. Those who genuinely serve the truth are gentle with it and humble. The truth need only be spoken and its force can be felt. When we defend a so-called truth by violence, we are not serving the truth but ourselves. We turn to violence because we are aware at some level of consciousness that the truth is not in us and we are, therefore, insecure with what we propose as the truth.

Those we define as our enemies are often not our enemies but simply those we cannot control, those who take options in life we did not, those who see an aspect of the truth to which we are blind. This is not to assume that there are no wicked people in the world. It is merely to state that there are far fewer than we suspect. Many of those we declare wicked are not wicked but different.

Nonviolence requires spiritual maturity. This is why prayer, as we discussed it in the previous chapter, is an important element in the achievement of nonviolence. The reason why nonviolence fails to work on many occasions is because others sense correctly that beneath the surface of the nonviolence there is hidden belligerence, a desire to control, or, at the very least, an assumption of moral superiority and self-righteousness.

Nonviolence is a humble approach to life, seeking to purify the self from the vanity which gets in the way of our happiness and the greed which makes us violent with one another.

Two assumptions which make violence seem advantageous must be looked at more carefully.

One of these is the notion that I am separate from the other, that I can hurt the other without injuring myself. We are more tightly bound together than this, Merton insists. In the act of inflicting pain on someone else, our hearts are poisoned. We sense shame, and rightly so. This is why when we choose to hurt others, we seek dark places, dungeons or windowless rooms. We harbor the very plans to do this in the shadows of our minds, concealing from others what we have done or intend to do.

Nonviolence, however, is done in the sunlight and the open air. We do not hide our actions from others because we know there is nothing disgraceful about them. Quite the contrary. If we do violence and many years later meet the victim, crippled, scarred, in pain, we do not feel proud about what we have done. If, however, we meet a person we have refused to injure, we are grateful for having left that person whole and healthy.

Augustine presupposed it was possible to create a distance between our intentions and our actions. Merton argues for something far more holistic and integrated. It is not only our intentions but the burden others bear because of them that must be addressed.

There is a second assumption that makes violence seem advantageous. Many people take for granted a world of zero sum possibilities, a world of scarcity and severe limits. In such a world, the more who share in the abundance, the less there is for others. We are not suggesting that there are absolutely no limits. After all, even the planet is a finite place. We do insist, however, that scarcity is often the result of violence already done against others. Scarcity is, in most instances, artificial and it is the direct result of greed and acquisitiveness.

This needs a word of explanation. We may not live in a world of zero sum possibilities, but in a world in which more is produced as more people come on the scene. Human creativity and need often generate opportunities that are not there when there are fewer who share in the abundance. In other words, we continue to expand the horizons of possibility and create ever new arrangements. Reality is not exhausted but augmented by the demands made upon it.

An example may help. One of the astonishing experiences of family life is its ability to absorb additional members into the circle even though it seemed there was no room for others. Parents who find that one or two children taxed their love and energy to the limit discover that there is love and energy sufficient for other children as they come on the scene. It is as though the love and energy expand to accommodate the additions.

We are not suggesting, foolishly, that there are no absolute limits. At a certain number, adding additional children to a family may be irresponsible. We do maintain that the number of those adequately and even generously able to be accommodated is far more than seems possible at first sight. Parents with large families report that, after a time, older children raise the younger, growing in maturity as they do so. The family learns to share and additional children enrich the lives of their siblings in new and unexpected ways.

I am, I must repeat, neither proposing large families as an ideal nor implying that there are no absolute limits. I am merely using an example to show that the limits are not as limiting as they seem at first sight.

The deficiency of vision and resiliency, of courage and creativity imprisons us into scarcity. The World Bank reports that a two percent redistribution of the world's grain supply would end malnutrition on the planet. It is difficult to imagine that artificiality and greed do not play a role in keeping us from implementing a relatively modest adjustment, granted the enormous benefits to human beings. To allow global malnourishment, under these circumstances, is an act of violence.

The world at large spends one million dollars a minute on weapons. Just one day out of that expenditure would save over a billion dollars. This massive waste is, indeed, the direct result of violence, fear and greed.

It is not the planet which is short on resources, but the human spirit. One year of allocating weapons budgets to schools and the arts, to medicine and clean water, to housing and urban renewal would benefit the human family enormously.

Early in the 1960's, John F. Kennedy gave his country a vision: Let us go to the moon before this decade is finished. The vision made possible an achievement which would not have been realized without it. Carl Sandburg, the American poet, tells us that nothing is possible without a dream.

If we envision a world in which weapons are necessary and in which some forms of violence are seen as virtues, then we must forever bear the burden and carry the cross of armaments and brutality. If we envision a world in which vulnerability and nonviolence are not dismissed as weaknesses, we create possibilities discarded as fantasies by those who cannot think otherwise.

None of this is easy. We must avoid the naiveté of supposing there are no shadows in human behavior, and we must not permit facile solutions and shallow analysis to undermine the credibility of what we propose.

Merton believed, correctly, that spirituality enhances and enriches our vision. Contemplation enables us to consider alternatives to the way things are and to the boundaries which are drawn too soon and too constrictively.

A discussion of the global dimensions of nonviolence can lead to undesirable consequences if we are not careful. We can become paralyzed before the massiveness of the problem and the limited power we have to create change. It is, therefore, necessary both to sketch out the global character of our predicament and to provide for individual initiative. If the problem is presented as overwhelming so that the individual is left with a sense of insignificance, we invite the evasion of personal responsibility rather than its engagement.

The world, in the long run, may be reformed more thoroughly by the nonviolence each of us makes part of ordinary life. Every time violence is rejected, the world is better, to that extent, forever. Simple, undramatic human actions form a critical mass which, at some point, effects enormous change. People may be willing to hear the message of Merton or to consider the points we are now making because the environment of human life has been altered in a thousand subtle and anonymous ways.

In an exercise of concreteness, I suggest ten strategies for nonviolence which every human being can implement easily in everyday life.

The first of these is to pay attention to people. Fewer things honor people as much or make them peaceful more readily or give them an experience of their worth as clearly as paying attention to them. People are starved, spiritually and emotionally malnourished, because there are so few willing to hear who they are and what they are trying to do with their lives.

The second is to verbalize human experience and to teach others to do this. Merton writes that the more inarticulate we are, the more likely it is that we might seek violence as a way of expressing ourselves. Articulateness does not mean literary grace, but putting into words our emotions and our life. We know how relieved we feel when we are searching and someone gives us the right word to say what we wish to communicate. Studies have shown that college graduates use physical violence less than secondary school graduates. I believe this may be due, in part, to the fact that college enhances our ability to verbalize. This, of course, does not mean that college graduates are morally superior. It does indicate that as we teach others to verbalize we help them turn from violence.

The third strategy is to reject excessive activity, accomplishment or success. There is something belligerent about frenetic action. Merton observes that we sometimes try to force meaning into our lives by compiling impressive résumés. An exaggerated concern with performance does violence to ourselves and to others. To say this is not to diminish the need for excellence or to counsel mediocrity. It is, however, to remind us that we do violence to ourselves more often than we realize. When people sense in us intensity, competitiveness, aggressiveness, they are intimidated and withdraw or take us on in a contest not unlike a military operation.

A fourth strategy is to practice contemplation. By contemplation, I mean life review, in silence, connecting our reflection with the ideals we have not achieved, making amends for things we regret, thanking God for the good we were given, the losses we survived, the love we received beyond all measure. Contemplation can be done when we are in an automobile or on a plane, in a waiting room, while eating alone, in the early morning, during a quiet walk, over coffee, in the stillness of the night. Modern life gives us many opportunities. A contemplative person brings tranquility into the world.

A fifth strategy is silence. Merton once observed that our silence is shattered not by speaking but by our eagerness and anxiety to be heard by others. Silence invites others to speak. By silence, I do not mean taciturnity. This is wordlessness which is a burden for others and may even appear hostile, threatening, unsettling. Genuine silence is creative and liberating. It invites communication and fosters it. Such silence brings peace to people.

Resisting consumerism is another practical strategy. A desperate need to possess is a form of violence. Excessive spending is a sign that one seeks the meaning of life in things. Henry David Thoreau reminds us in *Walden* that possessions possess the possessor, that Americans do not own their homes as much as their homes own them.

Losing and letting go is a seventh strategy. We are acculturated to go from success to success. Losing gracefully, even gratefully in terms of the long run, is a remarkable virtue. Chinese Taoism speaks of the rhythm of life which brings us on its own accord failure and achievement. Clutching at success when failure or letting go is necessary destroys us. My failure helps another win. My winning prepares me for failure. We become violent if we blame ourselves or others for our losses. Loss and gain come to all of us. What we call failure is, most often, not life failure but failure to reach a goal we artificially impose on life. In any case, life is not enriched by constant success. It is destroyed by it.

Scripture reading offers a further contribution to nonviolence. If people were to read Scripture reflectively for only five minutes a day, their lives would be enriched. No one is without five minutes a day of extra time. We need a standard by which to measure and mend our lives, a time-honored norm to inspire and motivate us. Scripture makes the norm, not whatever is presently fashionable, but what is truly enduring. It roots us and gives us peace in the turbulence of the passing crises we face.

Maintaining a sense of history is a ninth recommendation. We become frantic when we see life in the short run. If we look back on the frustrations of childhood or adolescence, we realize how unimportant many of them were. In the longer view of human history, or even of our personal histories, patterns of meaning emerge. The good does prevail.

A final strategy is to hold the conviction that people are basically good. One need only spend time at airport terminals to know how much people care for each other, miss each other, treasure each other. People must be reliable or else the gospel would not have lasted; Christ would have been forgotten. People create music and dance, art and families, playgrounds and schools, hospitals and gardens. If we believe people are basically evil, we are harsh and violent, pessimistic and cynical. Religious leaders may too often assume that people are not reliable and are not good. Much of the violence done in the name of religion—such an anomaly—has been premised on the idea that people are evil.

No one of these ten strategies is beyond any one of us. Together they take very little time. We are capable of every one of these strategies. They are concrete, practical, manageable, and they make a difference.

If we think these steps are of no account, let us merely ask ourselves what the world would be like if we all did them or even if many of us did them. It is well said that it is better to light a candle than to curse the darkness.

We have tried to show that nonviolence is not a luxury but an urgent concern. It is not at the margins of the spiritual life but at its core. It is not a fantasy, but it is literally the flesh and blood, the very life of our humanity.

For Reflection

- *Reflect on times in your life when you were violent or harsh with others, physically or verbally, by punishing silence or emotional aloofness. Consider the harm this may have caused. How do you feel about that now? Can you think of better ways you might have handled the problem?*

- *Reflect on times when you might have been severe and were not, times when you forgave in unexpected ways or reached out rather than retaliated. How do you feel about this now?*

- *Are there virtuous ways to conduct a war or execute a criminal? How would we react to hearing that Jesus approved of war in some circumstances and allowed or even recommended capital punishment?*

- *Do you believe the world has grown in its willingness to consider nonviolence?*

Closing Prayer

Gentle Jesus, crucified in agony, terror and mental torment, teach us to understand the mystery and love which led you to forgive your executioners. Teach us to appreciate the acceptance you offered to all the disciples who deserted you. Make our hearts gentle so that we may be strong, forgiving so that we may be made courageous, nonviolent so that we may reach our enemies as well as our friends. Amen.

DAY SIX
An Ocean Away

Coming Together in the Spirit

In the beginning of this retreat, we alluded to four
ecstatic experiences in Merton's life. During its course,
we described the apparition of his father that convinces
him he has a calling to the spiritual life. From this
moment forward, he is anchored in the belief that a better
life is possible for him, a settled life, a rooted existence.
He is in his eighteenth year of life when this occurs to
him; eight years later he will enter the Abbey of
Gethsemani.

Some seven years after the encounter with his
deceased father, he is in Cuba. We related this event in
our review of Merton's life. The issue before him in this
instance is not spiritual conversion but whether or not he
has a monastic vocation. At a liturgy, he hears a
congregation pray the Creed with the passionate:
"*Credo*...." This ecstasy is more auditory than visual. It is
not light in his room but voices in the Church which
strike him like a thunderclap, as he describes it. All fear
leaves him and he senses a beauty and certitude he has
never known. He is able now to enter the monastery. His
doubts disappear. It is 1940; he is in his twenty-fifth year
of life; a year later he is a monk.

These two occurrences are understandable to

conventional Catholics either in terms of their having happened at all or in their effect. They are, in a sense, calibrated to the mood and expectations of pre-conciliar Catholicism. In terms of their having happened, the pre-Vatican II Church believed strongly and with virtual unanimity in appearances. Lourdes and Fatima had a claim on Catholics at this time which is not replicated in later years.

In terms of their effect, these phenomena are all the more believable because the result is orthodox. A spiritual conversion and a monastic calling are widely endorsed choices in the Catholicism of the first half of the twentieth century.

The next two episodes could not have been assimilated by the Church before the Council. We shall describe them in these final two days of our retreat. They turn Merton, as a contemplative, to issues with a strong secular and political resonance and to awe before statues of Buddha. The former of these, secularity, we shall discuss in our final session. The latter is our concern now.

This incident occurs in the final week of Merton's life, on December 2, 1968, eight days before his death. He is in Sri Lanka and visits the Buddhist statues at Polonnaruwa. Let us do a flashback as Merton walks to the shrine. It will enable us to consider the enormity of the event and the astonishing change which had occurred in the life of our fifty-three-year-old monk.

We are, for a moment, in 1948, twenty years earlier. Merton has been a monk for seven years. He published two books in that year, neither of which have much good to say about Buddhism. One of these, *The Seven Storey Mountain*, refers to Buddhism as a nihilistic system, part and parcel of a false way of thinking. The second of these is even more searing in its attack on Buddhism. The book, *Exile Ends in Glory*, has a striking title, one which might describe Merton's life in a few words or, more specifically, the Asian journey and the death he is about to die. In any case, the book is not impressive, its title promising more than it delivers. Buddhism, in its Japanese expression, is described as superstitious, pagan, idolatrous. Statues of Buddha are referred to as blind and dead, with the implication that the religion that creates them is the same.

It is remarkable how far Merton journeys in the next twenty years. It is not himself alone but also the Church that travels a mighty distance in a short period of time. As late as 1959, Christians of other Churches were discounted as flawed and defective in their faith. Non-Christians would hardly be considered as even belonging to a religion, let alone one which might have something to offer Christians. Had someone told Merton as he finished *Exile Ends in Glory* that one day, he, a Cistercian monk, would stand in ecstasy before Buddha and see, in a flash, the meaning and purpose of his life, he would have dismissed such an idea as unworthy of further discussion.

We must not make light of the change which has occurred in our spiritual guide. In the 1940's Christ could be found properly in the Catholic Church alone. All other manifestations were to be discounted.

It is now 1968, December 2 to be exact. There is no intimation of how imminent are death and the end of the journey.

He is in Polonnaruwa and he approaches the statues of Buddha, not carved, he later reports, by ordinary mortals. The area is densely forested. It is then that it happens as he stands before the large, reclining figure. His description is electrifying, almost, one might conjecture, a description of being electrocuted. He is forcibly "jerked"—the word is his—out of ordinary experience. He feels an explosion inside him, clear, cleansing, liberating. In an instance, he realizes that there are no puzzles or problems in life. There are only emptiness and compassion.

Never before, Merton tells us, did beauty and spirituality become unified for him in so overwhelming a manner. He wonders about the future, is uncertain of its course but knows that he has seen the heart of reality, the core of the universe, the essence of life. He is far beneath the surface of things, carried beyond its shadows and disguises, as he calls them. He feels in his flesh and soul, clarity, purity, light, completion. He needs nothing else. It is fitting to be silent.

Merton shares this with us, as well as words can capture such a phenomenon. One gets the impression—it is not said, spoken—that further life is unnecessary, that the circle is complete, the journey finished. Such irony! That it should have reached a point of resolution in a context which once was judged undesirable, that serenity should be granted where formerly it would not have been sought, that light should be given in its most brilliant illumination just where previously only darkness would have been expected.

We need no further proof that the journey is not ours alone than Merton's life and pilgrimage. What was once contradictory is now seen as necessary; what was counterproductive becomes supportive; the enemy is the friend; the alien, the companion. The least of all emerges as God incarnate, as Christ with a face one does not at first recognize, as the disciples did not at Easter, but as Christ nonetheless now seen, as it were for the first time.

Defining Our Thematic Context

A constant concern of Merton is the answer to the question of where God dwells. There was a time in his life when God was an object of little concern. Even then, however, there were intimations and half-guesses, recollected in tranquility and crisis, when God got his attention. They are detailed in *The Seven Storey Mountain*.

When Merton becomes a Catholic, he finds God in a Church he had not anticipated. At Columbia University, he cannot envision God leading him to a Cistercian Abbey in Kentucky. He did not expect to find God in his writing or in social, prophetic protest. His negative references to Protestant Christianity in his autobiography did not prepare him to find God in all the Christian Churches as well as in the streets of Louisville.

Most astonishing is Merton's discovery of God in Asia and in Buddhism. If God could be present, active, fully available to him in this most remote and apparently impossible of all possible places, then surely God is everywhere. Merton learns what became for him a startling truth, that God is no less accessible to those who search in villages than in cathedrals, in metropolitan centers than in monasteries, in alternative Churches and religions, in marriage or celibacy, in the office or the choir. There are no privileged places. A burning bush may be a holy place as much as the temple, a manger as much as a synagogue, the Sea of Galilee as readily as a shrine. The sacred is everywhere. God may make use of a hotel in Rome or a home in Nazareth for an annunciation, a liturgy in Cuba or a mountain in Israel for a revelation, the streets of Kentucky or the hill country of Judaea for a visitation, the Buddhism of Asia or the Judaism of Palestine for a nativity, a death by electrocution in Thailand or a crucifixion near Jerusalem as an entrance into new life.

God dwells everywhere. This truth is easily proclaimed in the abstract and frequently denied in practice. It is credible as a doctrine but often rejected as a life experience.

One of the most crucial lessons Merton taught may well have been delivered in the last week of his life. His face, suffused with ecstasy in the forests and pilgrimage centers of Asia, and then twisted in pain as he dies in Bangkok, is the face of God, incarnate in Merton's life. It is the face of Christ, wearing the mantle of Buddhism and of death, looking beyond revelation to resurrection. Merton finds Easter in Polonnaruwa and in the Passover death which brings him beyond Gethsemani to paradise. God was present in every step of the journey because, of course, God dwells everywhere.

Opening Prayer

Blessed God, your servant Thomas once described contemplation as a country whose center is everywhere and whose boundaries are nowhere. Contemplation was for him not something to be discovered only on a long journey to exotic places but an experience encountered by standing still. By remaining where we are, we can make the present moment a sacrament of communion with you and compassion with one another. Make us contemplatives, a people of prayer, whose pilgrimage is not measured by geography but by grace, whose home is not built by human hands but discovered wherever you dwell. Live in us so that our hearts may become sacred places and so that all those we meet may know that God is present in our shared humanity, sacramentally concealed in the most ordinary of realities. You are the bread of our everyday living, consecrated and transformed by your presence into the wine of ecstasy and beatitude. Make us pilgrims on a journey such as this so that we may find you everywhere—even in the most startling of places, even in the routine experiences, and even in the hour of our death. Amen.

Retreat Session Six

We have much yet to explain. Turning East was one of the most provocative decisions of Merton's life. Many people turned from him as a guide after this. Even now his motives are questioned and his choice in this regard remains controversial.

Perhaps we should not have been surprised. It may not be a long step from nonviolence to the religions of the East. The Orient may have developed better—not perfectly, just better—a capacity for tolerance, a nonjudgmental approach to life, especially with regard to religious matters, a spirituality less militant and more resilient. To say this is not to ignore the limitations of Eastern religions but merely to underscore the fact that they bring with them different sensibilities, inclinations, tendencies.

Merton was alone through the early years of his life; we might call this the *Inferno* of his hopelessness and cynicism. There was death everywhere during these years. Merton's guides through the next stage, the *Purgatorio*, were the male companions of his Columbia years and his Abbey of Gethsemani community. They become his Virgil, pointing out to him possibilities he has not seen. The East was his Beatrice, leading him to the

Paradiso of the final ecstasy and his death.

The East stresses the "anima," the "feminine" (if you will and dare) side of the human psyche. In the intuitive and gentle dimensions of Oriental spirituality, Merton found the mother he never knew.

For a time in the monastery, Mother Church helped. It became the nurturing influence of his life. We showed earlier how the optimism and humanism, the community life and mystical orientation of Catholicism rescued the young Merton. The joy he finds in those first years in the abbey is the joy of the infant child with the mother who accepts fully and who gives the child companionship and love.

As Merton matures in the monastery, Mother Church becomes a more ambiguous influence. The Church would always be Merton's mother in some decisive and irreplaceable way. Now Merton sees harshness and arbitrary restriction, narrowness and even cruelty where once life had been so different. The dogmatism of Catholicism burdened Merton, its pretensions to have a truth which it did not possess, its need to define itself as superior to all systems and their judge, its self-indulgent preoccupation with its own infallibility, its crushing use of the law to imprison people in cages of compulsory celibacy and censorship. Merton loved what was best about Catholicism, but he began to criticize that which before he accepted as the natural course of events. He was like the mature adult who sees the limitations of the parent in ways that an earlier loyalty did not allow.

He turns East at just that point in his life when the anima or the feminine or even women are not discounted. It is not truth but compassion that he seeks. The nonviolence and the dialogues with Buddhists, the tea ceremonies and calligraphy, the writings of Chuang-tzu and the need to be a hermit, the preference of experience over theory, of contemplation over its form, of spirituality over Church structures, all of this attracts the feminine side of him.

There are escalating contradictions in his life now. He obeys the abbot but is frequently at odds with him; he loves the monastery but it seems insufficient; he chooses to remain a celibate but he wonders about the loss of romantic love in his life; he accepts the hierarchy of his Church but does not respect it—at least not as easily as he once did. He is ill frequently, with stress-related, psychosomatic maladies.

In Zen he encounters an experience which addresses the contradictions in a different context. Zen teaches him that the contradictions are not a problem, certainly not a sign of failure. The contradictions are not meant to be resolved but to be assimilated so fully that one goes beyond them. In a sense, the contradictions remain but one is simply not there anymore.

It is not very logical and it flies in the face of the animus or masculine side of each of our psyches. It may not be rationally compelling to think the way Zen suggests, but it seems right to Merton. This is not a truth that one can demonstrate with syllogisms and evidence, with proof and demonstrations. It is simply a truth which feels right for Merton. It is *his* truth. It must not be dismissed by him or taken away by another. He must see where this truth leads.

Zen pushes the contradictions to their ultimate limit where one must experience madness or unity. The irony lies in the fact that the contradictions are the essence of the unity and yet elude it.

Merton is weary as he turns to Zen, and Zen, with its utter simplicity, reaches his heart and renews his spirit.

Merton feared that the West had gone too far in adopting a Cartesian approach to life. The West tends to dualism, to the separation of good from evil, truth from error, self from others, God from creation, one religion from the rest. It concerns itself with decisive victories and precise doctrines.

Nonviolence is more congenial to an Oriental outlook on life because it invests less in the empirical self, the public self, the self in isolation. It seeks instead the real self beneath the surface, a self which is identified with others. It is on the empirical level that our contradictions and compulsions, eventually our belligerence, cluster. On the real level, there is harmony and peace.

The emergence of the real self requires suffering and sacrifice. We are obliged to take this journey to reality, to bear the pain and do the dying. Hence, there must be universal compassion. Compassion is the essence of spirituality and religion.

The mistake of the West lies in its attempt to find meaning in thinking and in the empirical self; the gift of the East is its insistence that meaning does not result from thinking, but from experience and that meaning is not for the self as an individual, but for everyone. We must, of course, not romanticize or idealize the East. It has its own obsessions and insufficiencies. For our purpose, however, it balances the West and comes with virtues that the West does not have.

Merton observes that the West transfers "being" into verbalism, mathematics and rationalization. The reason why nonviolence is difficult in concept as well as in practice is because it undermines the empirical self on which so much of Western culture is premised. The loss of this self is the beginning of wisdom and the essence of pacifism.

The Buddhist ability to make us compassionate rests upon its negation of distance and duality. Merton notes that this allows a rapprochement with Christianity.

Buddhism simply does not see alternative systems as false or even essentially different. In *Zen and the Birds of Appetite*, Merton states that Buddhism is a way of being in the world, not a doctrine. Buddhism is content to have the West define it as it wishes since all definitions are deficient.

Buddhism is frequently faulted because of its apparent indifference to social justice. Whatever one may think of this, Buddhism became, for Merton, an essential element in his social justice concerns.

An abiding sense of the unity possible when people are not violent or selfish was primary in bringing Merton to view Buddhism in such a way. Buddhism brought him a renewed sense of commitment. Evil in society ran deeper than its manifestations in experiences like Hiroshima or Auschwitz or Vietnam. These were only symptoms of a deeper need to be violent and of a compulsion to prefer the self. There will be further symptoms until the underlying problems are addressed. No investigation or reflection on why these atrocities occur will prevent their recurrence until the more profound aspects of the problem are confronted. Buddhism avoids the Western fascination with transforming persons and social institutions from the outside. It seeks to destroy the interior barriers of illusion that set up race or nation or even institutional religion as an absolute.

Buddhism involved Merton in reflection on the need to be sensitive to suffering in creation. His Christian commitment also helped. It focused his attention on the cross, where it is revealed that suffering is inevitable. The Resurrection makes it clear that suffering is evaded only if it is borne, since the Resurrection cannot happen except through suffering.

On a profound level, Buddhism and Christianity do

not disagree. In terms of experience, both systems converge. It is on the level of theory, Merton argued, that there are differences. The theory of Buddhism, however, is more critical to the West than it is to Buddhism. Thinking about experience is a Western preoccupation and an Oriental pastime.

Merton's turn East is linked with his growing spiritual maturity. Catholics whose vision was myopic saw Buddhism as a betrayal of Christianity. For Merton, it was necessary as a way of being Christian in a comprehensive manner. The stress on how different we are from one another is at the heart of our violent behavior. The truth of the matter lies in the similarity we have with one another.

Merton turns East as the evangelical and Franciscan poverty he always prized came to mean even more to him. Merton lived many years without material possessions. After a time, this sacrifice in the name of poverty did not require enough of him. He found a more profound poverty in denying himself the security of remaining always as he was before, of not risking, of repeating patterns of behavior and productivity which assured him popular or ecclesiastical approval. Merton speaks of letting go, of not clinging to possessions or approbation. If I cling to something, he notes, just because society expects it of me, it will do me no good. He writes, in a letter to his friend James Loughlin, that life cannot and ought not be fully consistent.

Merton brings together his nonviolence and his search for the spiritual wisdom of the East in a book entitled *Original Child Bomb*. The title comes from the Japanese name for the atomic bomb detonated over Hiroshima.

Merton had been writing about Gandhi and Martin Luther King, about Zen and Chinese Taoism. This led him to examine the myths or received truths which drive our culture and are accepted without challenge, analysis or critical review. These myths explain why we used the bomb.

It is foolish for any culture to assume it is not profoundly influenced by a myth system. Such a denial is a myth in itself.

One of America's enduring myths is the engineering or efficiency myth. It is difficult for us not to engineer what is possible and use what is efficient. This myth made the unleashing of the atomic bomb an item of great urgency. The bomb is a model of engineering genius and it is an extraordinarily efficient killer. It may, of course, be argued that the bomb saved lives, since an invasion of Japan would have entailed a staggering loss of life on both sides. Merton is troubled by the lack of moral and ethical discussion in the decision to use the bomb. There is, in its place, a great deal of awe about the ingenuity of the weapon, its unbelievable firepower, its efficiency.

A second myth is the control myth. This myth brings us satisfaction when we and others are in absolute control. The control myth may operate in government or Church, in the lives of parents or professors, of physicians or spouses The bomb is a very intimidating weapon, fearsome beyond description. It gives a nation that possesses it tremendous control over others. The bombing of Hiroshima brings submission from Japan, but also compliance from other nations. It punishes Japan for its attack on the United States. This punishment becomes an object lesson to potential aggressors. It keeps people in line.

The progress myth is also operative. This assures us that endless technological and human improvement is possible. It leads us to believe that all our miscalculations are reversible. We assume that even if problems arise from our weaponry, they can be solved.

The affluence myth convinces us that possessions are a sign of superiority and that security can be derived from something we own. Applied to warfare, it engenders the notion that a decisive military victory proves that God or moral rectitude is with us. If we have a weapon no one else does, we must be a great nation. America is a great nation, but not necessarily for the reasons we sometimes offer.

A fifth myth is the necessity for unconditional surrender of enemies. This is premised on the illusion that the adversary is totally evil and not truly human. One must, therefore, destroy not only the potential to wage war but also the very spirit of the opponent. Such thinking makes a nuclear weapon a legitimate option. It further allows the foe only abject capitulation, with no guarantees, conditions, or reservations, even if these are reasonable and humane.

There are other myths, but these may help us understand how our policies as a people or our behavior as individuals may appear necessary even when they are not. The purpose of exposing these myths and explaining them is not necessarily to argue one way or another about the correctness of the strategy adopted. It is rather to reveal the fact that those who plan a course of action are not as rational as they suppose.

Merton would not have been capable of analyzing Western culture in this manner without a developed sensitivity for the East, its culture and spirituality, its writers and religious people.

Since there is no operative myth of nonviolence in the West, nonviolence does not seem possible, desirable or imperative. It is true that the Christ story could provide such a myth, but the West has tended to prefer the notion of Christ as triumphant victor, king, ruler, lord, judge, avenger. This reading of the life of Christ led to crusades and inquisitions, to belligerent hierarchies and dominating legal systems, to infallible rulers and councils which anathematized. There are, we know, more gentle interpretations of Christ given by saints and compassionate people, by those who nurtured life and preserved it even when it was the life of adversaries. These more benign views of Christ, however, were not strong enough to create a myth of nonviolence.

Merton roots nonviolence in Eastern spirituality and in the better versions of the life of Christ. Indeed, Buddhism may allow us to see the gentle and nonviolent Christ more clearly.

People sense an imperative to do certain things in a culture because the assumptions or myths, the symbols or social forces move them powerfully in a certain direction. Americans who prize freedom, clearly one of the effective myths in our culture, who believe that free choice is of the essence of human life, seldom realize how often that freedom is restricted by cultural myths unconsciously accepted.

Americans give a high priority to freedom in the external order of their lives; freedom of the spirit, internal freedom, may be more limited. If we are not alert, we can internalize our bondage. Many examples in world literature and history extol those who, though literally imprisoned, kept their spirits free. There are less admirable manifestations in everyday life of people who possess their freedom and options in the external order but who are in bondage to cultural obsessions, hidden persuaders and frenetic compulsions.

Original Child Bomb is Merton's account of the American decision to drop the first atomic bomb and of the myths which drove that decision. Merton refers to how often religious language was used to describe this destructive weapon. It is called a "child" that will usher in an era of peace. Winston Churchill is informed of its existence with the code message: "Babies satisfactorily born." This engine of death is described in terms of life; the belligerent weapon is celebrated as a path to peace. The name for the atomic device exploded in New Mexico to prove the viability of the weapon was "Trinity." The blinding brightness of the explosion leads an official witness to cry out: "Lord, I believe. Help thou my unbelief." An American admiral (Leahy), who is not convinced such a weapon will work, is called a "doubting Thomas." The *U.S.S. Indianapolis* takes the U-235 in a lead bucket to Tinian Island where the bomb will be constructed. The ship's instructions read that, should it be attacked and in danger of sinking, the uranium must be saved before any human life. In cultures driven by the technological myth, the artifact or product, the machine or assembly line are more valuable than people. The servants of the U-235 on the *Indianapolis* are expected to be sacrificed for the idol. After the bomb is delivered, the plane which took it to its target, the *Enola Gay*, heads for Tinian while Hiroshima is engulfed in nuclear fires. The code name for the return flight is "Papacy."

For Reflection

- *How do you respond to Merton's approach to Buddhism?*

- *Are there myths in your own life which exert a strong influence on your behavior?*

- *How do you interpret the life of Jesus? Which were the dominant values and concerns of his life?*

- *Are there ways other religions were presented to you in the past which you would no longer accept?*

- *Was God described when you were young in terms that you would no longer accept?*

Closing Prayer

Loving Creator, you who made all human hearts and are present in all human cultures, help us to find you in all the forms you take and in all the ways people seek you. Merciful Savior, you who redeemed the world and loved the human family, enable us to sense your healing presence in those who seek to be rescued from the forces which bring death instead of life. Holy Spirit, you who inspire human minds and souls with grace and goodness, teach us to find you in all those whose lives are lifted up by your nearness. Amen.

DAY SEVEN
A World Regained

Coming Together in the Spirit

By his own account, it happened at the corner of
Fourth and Walnut. The location does not have a ring to
it. The fact that it occurred in Louisville, Kentucky, helps
to define it but does not add glamour or impressive name
recognition. Other ecstasies took place in Rome and
Havana. There was also Polonnaruwa, hardly a
household word. Yet, it is in Sri Lanka and Asia; it sounds
exotic, remote. There is an appeal to it. But Fourth and
Walnut is pedestrian, commonplace. It reminds one of a
police report rather than a theophany. It suggests a
direction one might give a taxi driver rather than a
location where God would choose to meet us.

Yet, perhaps, this is exactly as it should be. Merton
labored in his life to convince us that God is everywhere
and that the spiritual life is for everyone. One need not go
to Europe or Asia, to Cuba or a Cistercian monastery to
find God. God is present as the traffic light changes at
Fourth and Walnut in downtown Louisville. The crowds
are there on business, not on a journey to the promised
land. They are crossing a street, not a sea where the
waters part. There is no burning bush here, only a red
traffic light. It is ordinary in the extreme. It is not the stuff
from which myths are made or the environment one

would choose for a major religious event.

Yet that is where it happened.

The year is 1958; Merton gives us the exact date, March 18. It is his seventeenth year in the monastery, the beginning of the last decade of his life. This is where Merton is on the calendar of his existence, so to speak. Psychologically and spiritually, we need other coordinates and measures to know where he is.

The decade after the 1948 publication of *The Seven Storey Mountain* was one of profound redirection. It does not even approximate, however, the turbulent change of his final decade, 1958 to 1968. Our concern now is 1958, the first year of the last decade.

Merton "left the world," as it is said, in 1941. His autobiography, seven years later, celebrates that fact. The world he renounces is his audience. It seeks him out, it pursues him after 1948 and he is not reluctant. He needs the world for his spirituality and fears it even as he paradoxically invites it. He requires its presence and even approval, but cannot admit this to himself.

There are two issues he is not able to settle in this decade. One concerns his writing; the other his need to keep contact with the world. Both issues have the potential to destroy his monastic commitment, to end his life as a contemplative. There are no wise guides to serve as mentors to navigate him through these perilous waters. He has lost three fathers who might have helped. His parent, Owen, is dead; his guardian, Bennett, will not communicate; his first abbot, Frederic Dunne, whom Merton described as more kind to him than anyone else had ever been, dies suddenly. Abbot Dunne suggested Merton write his autobiography, protected him against those who felt this violated Cistercian custom, and handed him the first copy of the book in the month before he, Dunne, died.

Merton writes furiously in the decade after *The Seven Storey Mountain*. He is delighted and tormented. The delight comes from the sheer joy of composing, the magic and miracle of words. Publishing a book is like fathering a child. The book is generated by the author but has a life of its own. The writing has a strange effect on him. It becomes a sacramental experience, bringing him God, nurturing his contemplative calling. But he is tormented. All this notoriety may lead to vanity; the monastery is no longer the quiet abbey it once was now that one of its monks is a world celebrity; some monks are resentful at the way Merton has disturbed their lives; the writing seems to violate the rule of silence and the point of becoming a Cistercian. In 1958, the issue is still not settled.

The other painful issue concerns contact with the world. Merton is moving toward a major investment of his life in social justice. He spends a seemingly inordinate amount of time in correspondence, in reading news articles people send him and books he orders from local libraries. He is as much in the world at large in his thoughts and concerns as he is in the monastery. Is this a betrayal? Is he being dishonest with himself and others, proclaiming to be what he is not? What about the guilt, the punishment? Is life becoming too easy? Has he paid the price for so many misdeeds? Is he purified from his transgressions? Is he trying to have more than he ought, the security of the monastery and the allure of a creative life in the world? Is he seeking to hold on to the world but without paying the price of the risk and courage required to live such a life? Is the monastery now a place of convenience, a shelter from what his contemporaries in the world must face if they choose to live a life of fame and influence? Is all this contact with people in their ordinariness, in the sometimes trivial concerns of daily life, in their frustrations—is all this in accord with his vocation, with his public definition of himself as a contemplative monk?

He cries out in exasperation. If the world is his problem, if this is why he came to the monastery, why does he have the same problems he once had in the world? Why is he so much the same person after so many years in the monastery, after so much prayer and sacrifice, so much anonymity and seclusion, so much fasting and penance?

This is the monk who waits for a traffic light to change on the corner of Fourth and Walnut on March 18, 1958.

He looks at the people around him and realizes how deep is his love for all people. He feels as though he were waking from a dream, a dream of separateness from the human race, an illusion in which he was special and different. Merton states that his autonomous distance from others is not real; it is artificial, juridical.

He knows he has made a terrible mistake. The glory of human life is not in what differentiates us from others but in what unites us inseparably to them. It is not being a monk which matters; it is being a part of the human race. God did not become incarnate as a monk but as a human being. The glory of God Incarnate is the human face of Jesus. God Emmanuel is God as part of our family, not God as different, distant, autonomous, aloof, special.

The book in which this description occurs is the brilliantly entitled *Conjectures of a Guilty Bystander*. It is a book in which the guilt of being an observer rather than a participant in human affairs will be absolved by the revelation we are describing.

The language is charged because the emotional intensity is overpowering.

Merton speaks of being overwhelmed. He is in a shopping district and realizes in a flash that these people belong to him and he to them. There is no such thing as a holy existence which can be holy at a distance from people. A monastery is unfortunately too often a fortress against the world. God does not use the Incarnation as a bulwark against people.

Such a deception! To think that a consecrated life makes people a different species. Such arrogance!

Holiness is rooted in everyday life and in secular, worldly living. It is "preposterous"—the word is Merton's—to think that monks are better than shoppers.

Merton wants to laugh out loud in joy as he feels the liberation. He thanks God in a mantra, a litany, saying repeatedly that God has made him like everyone else and, therefore, he must be grateful. Thank God, thank God! Seventeen years of illusion come to an end at Fourth and Walnut. To be human is all one needs to win the cosmic sweepstakes.

Merton sees human faces shining with sunlight. He sees in this light the secret beauty of the human heart, the core of its reality where neither sin nor evil can enter and contaminate. The essential purity of people is not forfeited by their misdeeds, still less by their living out a human existence. Such folly! If people could see themselves as they are, they would kneel and "worship" each other.

God preserves the pure diamond of our hearts. The invisible light of heaven bathes this diamond in brilliance. Every corner of the earth is the gate of heaven.

Once again, ecstasy settles a problem for Merton. He crosses Fourth and Walnut and passes over into a new life. The final decade of his life will be free of guilt about being who he is, a writer. He will give himself to social justice and contemplation, to politics and prayer, to liturgy and life.

Looking Back

We have traveled together a long journey in a short time. Perhaps this description fits our entire lives. In any case, it seems an appropriate account of what we have experienced.

We entered the heart of a man unlike us in many ways, it seemed. We found there the heart of a brother, someone so like us that he belonged to our family. He was almost a mirror of ourselves. Perhaps this is how the disciples came to know Jesus.

In Merton, we could feel the shock and vibrancy of the twentieth century. He helped us be at home with our own lives, our own time, our contemporaries, our friends and our adversaries. He took from us the strangeness and alienation which made us exiles in our own lives.

Along the way, we learned about prayer and nonviolence, the East and spirituality, ecstasy and human experience. We traveled to Europe and the Western Hemisphere, to Asia and Kentucky, to Rome and New York City and Louisville. We walked with Merton his first steps of life, stood nearby as his parents died, heard his stories of visions and temptations.

Our mentor shared his poetry and journals, his heartaches and graces. He took us to Gethsemani and Sri Lanka, to Fourth and Walnut and Hiroshima, introduced us to Gandhi and Buddhism, to Zen and Catholicism.

For Reflection

There are questions yet to ponder. They are questions to take on our way, to contemplate on the journey beyond this juncture.

- *What have been the most meaningful moments in your life?*

- *Are these moments sacred in themselves or do they require the Church's endorsement of them before you see them as holy?*

- *In your everyday life, who have been saints for you?*

- *Do you believe that God preserves our inner purity in spite of our sins?*

- *What words would you use to describe Merton's life?*

- *What words would describe your own life?*

- *What would being in a monastery add to your life? What would it take from it?*

- *There were priests during the lifetime of Jesus and there were monks in communities around the Dead Sea. What do you think of the fact that God became incarnate not as a priest or monk, but as a layperson and carpenter?*

- *If we believe God is everywhere, why do we have such difficulty in finding God in our own life?*

- *Think of ten very ordinary things we do and reflect on their meaning and their sacredness, their ability to make our lives work and their capacity to bring us to God.*

Deepening Your Acquaintance

We have met on the journey. We have talked of many things, but mostly of God and each other. It is time to part. Such a time always arrives, even when we are not ready and willing.

On some level, all the moments remain. They become part of us and we bring them with us to paradise. It is only then that we see clearly how much God was present at every turn, only then that we understand how near Christ was and is.

For Further Reading

Merton: A Film Biography. Videocassette. Palisades Home Video.

Merton, Thomas. *New Seeds of Contemplation*. Trappist, Ky.: The Abbey of Gethsemani, 1961.

_____ . *The Seven Storey Mountain*. New York: Harcourt Brace, 1948.

Mott, Michael. *The Seven Mountains of Thomas Merton*. Boston: Houghton Mifflin, 1984.

Padovano, Anthony. *Conscience and Conflict: A Trio of One-Actor Plays*. New York: Paulist Press, 1988.

_____ . *Contemplation and Compassion: Thomas Merton's Vision*. White Plains, N.Y.: Peter Pauper Press, 1984.

_____ . *The Human Journey: Thomas Merton, Symbol of*

a Century. Garden City, N.Y.: Doubleday, 1982

_____ . *Winter Rain: A Play*. Videocassette. Paulist Press.